NATIVE TRIBES OF THE
NORTHEAST

Michael Johnson

WORLD ALMANAC® LIBRARY

Please visit our web site at: **www.worldalmanaclibrary.com**
For a free color catalog describing World Almanac® Library's list
of high-quality books and multimedia programs, call 1-800-848-2928 (USA)
or 1-800-387-3178 (Canada). World Almanac® Library's fax: (414) 332-3567.

Library of Congress Cataloging-in-Publication Data available upon request from publisher.
Fax (414) 336-0157 for the attention of the Publishing Records Department.

ISBN 0-8368-5612-0

This North American edition first published in 2004 by
World Almanac® Library
330 West Olive Street, Suite 100
Milwaukee, WI 53212 USA

For Compendium Publishing
Contributors: Michael Johnson and Duncan Clarke
Editor: Michael Burke
Picture research: Michael Johnson and Simon Forty
Design: Tony Stocks/Compendium Design
Maps: Mark Franklin

World Almanac® Library editor: Gini Holland
World Almanac® Library graphic designer: Steve Schraenkler

Picture credits
All artwork (other than maps) reproduced by kind permission of Richard Hook. All photographs are by Michael Johnson or supplied from his collection unless credited otherwise below. Particular thanks are due to the staff of Royal Albert Memorial Museum and Art Gallery, Exeter, Devon, U.K., for assistance and access to its exhibts, archives, and excellent collections, and to Bill Yenne for material of his own and from his collection. Much of the material in this book appeared as part of *The Encyclopedia of Native Tribes of North America* by M. J. Johnson and R. Hook, published by Compendium Publishing Ltd. in 2001.

Alan Mitchell Collection (photography by Simon Clay): p. 9; Spooner Hall, University of Kansas Collection, Lawerence, Kansas: p. 14; Horniman Museum, London, U.K.: p. 15; Hudson's Gallery: pp. 42, 45; Mark J. Sykes Collection: p. 25; M. J. Johnson Collection (photography by Simon Clay): p. 34 (above); Pitt Rivers Museum, Oxford, U.K.: p. 37 (below); Richard Green Collection (photography by Simon Clay): pp. 10 (left), 29 (left) 29 (left); Royal Albert Memorial Museum and Art Gallery: pp. 1, 4, 17 (above), 18 (below left, above and below right), 32, 34 (below), 38; St. Michael Mission, Fort Totten, North Dakota: p. 33; University Museum of Archaeology and Anthropology, Cambridge, U.K.: pp. 18 (above left), 20 (below); J. E. Whitney, St. Paul, Minnesota: p. 37 (above right); Bill Yenne: p. 30; National Museums and Galleries on Merseyside, Liverpool, U.K.

Printed in the United States of America

1 2 3 4 5 6 7 8 9 08 07 06 05 04

Cover: Indian chief of Six Nations (Iroquois), c. 1860s. He wears a beaded cap with feathers and horsehair and a beaded baldric over a buckskin jacket.

Previous Page: Ceremonial hooded cape of the mid-nineteenth century. Hoods of fur, skin, and later of cloth were known throughout the North, Subarctic, and Northeast areas, particularly among Algonkian-speaking groups. They gave protection against the weather and some had magico-religious significance. Those with ears like this have been recorded in an area from the Penobscot of Maine west to the Plains Cree. The decoration on the front is similar to that found on examples of East Cree manufacture around James Bay, Canada.

Contents

Introduction

For thousands of years, the people known today as Native Americans or American Indians have inhabited the whole of the Americas, from Alaska to the southernmost tip of South America. Most scholars and anthropologists think that the ancestors of Native peoples came to the Americas from Asia over a land mass connecting Siberia and Alaska. These first Americans may have arrived as long as 30,000 years ago, although most historians estimate that this migration took place 15,000 years ago.

According to this theory, Paleo-Indians (*paleo*, from a Greek word meaning "ancient") migrated over many years down through an ice-free corridor in North America, spreading out from west to east and southward into Central and South America. In time, they inhabited the entire Western Hemisphere from north to south. Their descendants became the many diverse Native peoples encountered by European explorers and settlers.

"INDIANS" VS. "NATIVE AMERICANS"

Christopher Columbus is said to have "discovered" the Americas in 1492. But did he? Columbus was not the first European to visit what became known as the New World; Viking mariners had sailed to Greenland and Newfoundland almost five hundred years before and even founded short-lived colonies. Using the word "discovered" also ignores the fact that North America was already inhabited by Native civilizations whose ancestors had "discovered" the Americas for themselves.

When Columbus landed on an island he called San Salvador (Spanish for "Holy Savior"), he thought he had reached China or Japan. He had sailed west intending to get to the East—to Asia, or the fabled "Indies," as it was often called by Europeans of the time. Although he landed in the Bahamas, Columbus never really gave up on the idea that he had made it to the Indies. Thus when Native people first encountered Columbus and his men in the islands off Florida, the lost explorer called them "Indians." The original names that each tribal group had already given to themselves usually translate into English as "the people" or "human beings." Today, some Native people of North

Above: **Huron porcupine-quilled pouch. The northeastern tribes were renowned for their quillwork.**

America prefer to be called "American Indians," while others prefer "Native Americans." In this book, Native peoples will be referred to by their tribal names or, in more general cases, as "Indians."

Today's Indians are descended from cultures of great historical depth, diversity, and complexity. Their ancient ancestors, the Paleo-Indians, developed beliefs and behavior patterns that enabled them to survive in unpredictable and often harsh environments. These early hunter-gatherers had a close relationship with the land and a sense of absolute and eternal belonging to it. To them, everything in their world—trees, mountains, rivers, sky, animals, rock formations—had "spirit power," which they respected and placated through prayers and rituals in order to ensure their survival. These beliefs evolved over time into a fascinating and diverse series of creation stories, trickster tales, songs, prayers, and rituals passed down to and practiced by tribes throughout North America. Although many Indians today practice Christianity and other religions as well, many of their traditional songs, stories, dances, and other practices survive, on reservations and in areas where substantial tribal groups still live.

A CONTINENT OF CULTURES

Long before the Europeans arrived, important Indian cultures had already developed and disappeared. The ancient Adena and Hopewell people, for example, built a number of extraordinary burial mounds, and later even large towns, some of whose remains can still be seen at sites in the Midwest and South. These cultures were themselves gradually influenced by Mesoamerican (pre-Columbian Mexican and Central American) farming cultures based on growing maize (Indian corn), beans, and squash. They became the Mississippian culture from 700 A.D. The great spread of language groups across the North American continent also points to a rich Indian history of continual movement, invasion, migration, and conquest that took place long before European contact.

By the time the first European explorers and colonists set foot in North America, Indians had settled across the vast continent into different tribal groups and cultures that were active, energetic, and continually changing. American Indians were skilled in exploiting their particular

<aside>

U.S. INDIAN POPULATION

There is no record of the number of Indians living north of the Rio Grande before Europeans came. A conservative estimate of Indian population made by ethnographer James Mooney is about 1,250,000 for the late sixteenth century, before the founding of Jamestown and Plymouth. Others have suggested figures as high as six million, although two to three million might be more realistic. The highest concentrations of people were in the coastal regions: the Atlantic slope in the East, along the Gulf of Mexico in the South, and in California in the West. Indians living in these areas also suffered the most from European diseases and from conflict with European colonists. Population figures for the twentieth century vary considerably, due mainly to U.S. government criteria used to determine who is or is not an Indian. Also, the U.S. Bureau of Indian Affairs (BIA), the official bureaucracy in charge of the remaining Indian lands and federal services to Indians, has few relations with Indians in certain states. Thus the BIA's population figures tend to be lower than those reported by the U.S. Census. In 1950 the BIA reported 396,000 enrolled Indians, of whom 245,000 were resident on reservations. The U.S. Census reported 827,108 Indians in 1970 and 1,418,195 in 1980. Census 2000 recorded 2,409,578 respondents who reported as American Indian or Alaskan Native only and identified a single tribe of origin.

</aside>

Above: **Wigwams of the Southern New England Algonkians, reconstructed at the American Indian Archaeological Institute, Washington, Connecticut.**

environments in a multitude of ways developed over time. They were also good at incorporating new methods and technologies from other peoples. When Europeans came, many Indians adapted the newcomers' technology to their own way of life, incorporating, for example, the horse, the rifle, money, beads, fabric, steel implements, and European-style agriculture into their own traditional cultures. In many cases, however, the benefits of European influence were eventually overshadowed by the displacement or outright destruction of traditional Native life.

WHAT THIS BOOK COVERS

The purpose of this book is to give some relevant facts about each of the main tribes native to North America, north of the Rio Grande. There are brief historical sketches of the tribes, descriptions of tribal language relationships and groups, and accounts of traditional cultures, tribal locations, and populations in early and recent times. Today's political boundaries were not recognized by Indians on their original lands: Their markers were on the land; their borders were the shifting lines of hunting, gathering, and farming areas used and fought over by different tribes. For ease of reference, however, tribal locations given here refer to modern U.S. and Canadian place names.

NORTHEASTERN WOODLANDS

The Woodland culture dominated the Northeast. This area comprises the central plain between the Atlantic Ocean and the Allegheny and Appalachian mountain ranges, the rich-soiled river areas of the Ohio and Mississippi Valleys, the Great Lakes, and the coastal Maritimes (Canada's Atlantic provinces). This is a huge land of forests, both deciduous and evergreen, which (from north to south) abounds in birch, elm, dogwood, oak, hickory, southern pine, mountain ash and eventually, in the Southeastern area, includes mangrove swamp.

This region is home to many different cultural traditions, including distinctive survival skills, arts and crafts, and religious practices. Slash-and-burn agriculture, an influence from Mesoamerica, was universally used except in the areas farthest north.

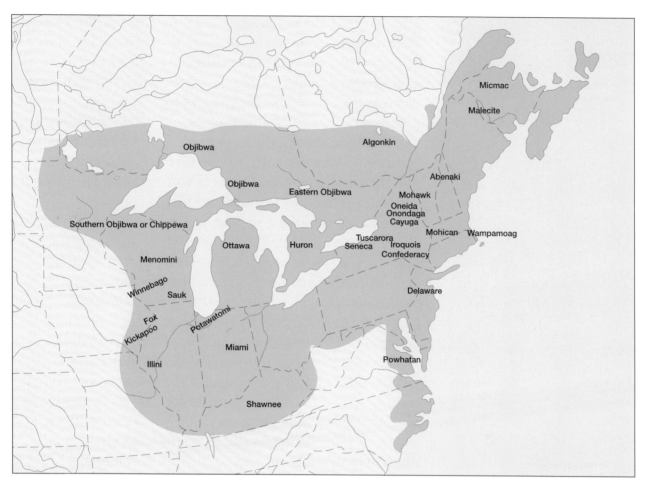

The first Mesoamerican influences arrived in about 2000 B.C.; crude pottery and polished stone objects that have been found may date from this period. Later, more sophisticated Mound Builder cultures flourished, such as the Adena of Ohio and Kentucky, 800 B.C.–A.D. 200. These people are noted for burying their dead in, at first, natural mounds and later in burial mounds built by humans and surrounded by earth walls. Their famous Serpent Mound in Ohio is perhaps the most spectacular of these. This culture also produced domesticated plants, squashes, pumpkins, and cord-marked pottery. The Hopewell culture, after 100 B.C., further developed mound-oriented burial ceremonies and death ritual cults. The Hopewell people also created pottery, stone carving, and realistic art forms of birds, animals, and humans in clay, copper, mica, and shell.

The last cultural complex was the Mississippian, which re-entered the old Hopewell area at Cahokia (across the Mississippi River from modern St. Louis) and

Above: **The area covered in this book stretches from the north Atlantic coast to the Great Lakes and adjacent southern Canada.**

Above: **Indian doll, c. 1850. Great Lakes area, probably Ottawa or Ojibwa. A European trade doll dressed by the Indians as a warrior figure with facial tattoos, braided hair, feathers, cloth skirt, breechcloth, moccasins, and leggings and decorated with ribbonwork and beadwork.**

Fort Ancient (in southwestern Ohio) from around A.D. 700 until the time of the European invasion. This late "Temple Mound" period is characterized by intensive agriculture of a Mesoamerican type, relatively superior pottery, palisaded and fortified villages, and flat-topped pyramid mounds (as at Cahokia, which in its heyday was a city of about 25,000 people). During the fifteenth century a religious cult, known as the Southern Cult, and its associated ritual objects were grafted onto the existing temple platform traditions.

Although this culture barely survived to the time of European contact, the earliest white adventurers saw the remnants of it. Hernando De Soto's Spanish expedition of 1540 encountered the Mississippian culture as it survived among the Creek, Cherokee, and Natchez tribes of the Southeast, with their class system of nobility and commoners, their distinctive appearance using ear circles and gorget decorations (ornamental throat guards), and the ritual colors they employed: red for war and white for peace. The northern offshoot of this culture formed the Woodland pattern, which, in various local phases, would give birth to late Woodland culture.

The Iroquoian Hurons were the northernmost people to practice extensive agriculture, albeit crude, and their Feast of the Dead, witnessed by French Jesuit missionaries, is related to Mississippian culture traits. The Iroquois were typical representatives of Woodland culture, with their belief in a Creator and in *orenda,* the life force, which embodied the health and creativity of all nature, opposed by the spirits of evil and destruction.

The other major Woodland group, the Algonkians, also had a worldview characterized by an overwhelming fear of sorcery. They believed in a pantheon of destructive spirits such as the Windigowan, cannibal ice giants. To the Algonkians, the whole natural world was inhabited by spirit forms. Their supreme spirit was Manito or Midemanido, and their great culture hero was Nanabush. Both Iroquois and Algonkian religions would be modified over the years by European influence and contact with Christianity.

Wood and bark were important material resources for the forest Indians. They used them to fashion canoes of birch or elm bark, and to construct toboggans (an Algonkian word), as well as bows, arrows, clubs, baskets, containers, spoons, bowls, pestles, mortars, cradleboards, drums, lacrosse racquets, and ball game sticks. Wigwams (from an Eastern Abenaki word), a common type of shelter, were bark or reed mats sewn to a frame of saplings that had been tied together with spruce roots.

EUROPEAN CONTACT

The Indian peoples of eastern North America experienced a long period of white contact, and over time their way of life was significantly affected by the invading Europeans. Many tribes, especially along the coast, were entirely or largely destroyed by European diseases. As interior tribes subsequently adopted both the remnants of these weakened tribes and white captives, there was greater mixing and marrying among tribes. This led to a "hybrid" quality (mixing diverse elements) to northeastern Indians' material culture and clothing decoration. Before the end of the seventeenth century, cloth, beads, silver, trade tomahawks, guns, thread, wool, and metal trade goods were known to Indians as far west as the Mississippi River.

Indian dress in the Northeast was modified by these European influences, but in pre-contact times hide tunics were probably worn by men, slit skirts by women, with a wide use of wampum shell for beads and decoration. However, European cloth and trade goods were adopted so quickly that by the eighteenth century, Indians in close association with whites used broadcloth and calico for their clothing. The Woodland tribes were expert workers of porcupine quills, natural fibers, moose hair, paint, and later, beadwork to decorate all manner of articles with symbolic imagery from their myths and stories. In the nineteenth century, heavy floral-design beadwork became popular for dance costumes, as did cut-and-fold ribbonwork, which still remains popular.

Intertribal warfare was common, and bitter wars during the colonial period were in part continuations of ancient conflicts between tribes. Thus, Indian tribes often aligned themselves with various colonial forces for

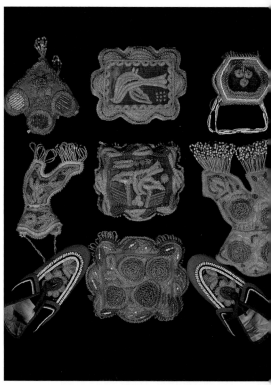

Above: **Interaction with the European settlers eventually encouraged the Indians to produce material for tourists and sightseers. This collection of Iroquois products was for the nineteenth-century souvenir trade.**

Below: **The tribes of the Northeast are particularly noted for their beadwork—especially their floral beadwork designs as on these Ojibwa vest and leggings of the late nineteenth century.**

their own political objectives, employing the often-used political strategy which declares that the enemy of one's enemy is a good ally. Similarly, the Europeans often sought alliances with Indians in their ongoing wars for colonial dominance. Opposed to this, some Indian holy men preached against war and evil brought by whites.

Despite centuries of conflict with whites and large-scale destruction of their population, the Woodland people have survived in many areas to this day. A few mixed-descent people still claim coastal Algonkian ancestry, the Iroquois still occupy fractions of their old territory, and the Ojibwas are still numerous in the northern fringes of the Great Lakes states and adjacent parts of Canada. The southern Woodland tribes mostly found their way to Oklahoma and have fully participated in the Pan-Indian (involving many different tribes) cultural revival of recent times. Many have lost a major part of the old traditional culture through mass movement away from family ties on the reservations and into the cities. The force of tradition, however, remains strong for many. For example, some Kickapoo Indians (originally from the southern Great Lakes area) have maintained a semblance of their old forest life in their new Mexican environment, and the Mesquakies, or Fox Indians, purchased their own lands to be free of government influences. Both groups retained a distinctively Woodland culture until quite recent times.

Right: **Ojibwa Snowshoe Dance, at the first snowfall, painted by George Catlin, 1835–1837. This was the thanksgiving to the Great Spirit for giving the people the ability to continue hunting in winter, when they could travel on their snowshoes.**

TRIBES OF THE NORTHEAST

Tribe	Meaning of name	Tribe	Meaning of name
Abenaki	easterners	Niantic	at a point of land on a river
Algonkin	place of spearing fish (or eels)	Nipissing	at the lake
Brotherton	English name	Nipmuc	freshwater fishing place
Cayuga	–	Nottoway	adders
Conoy	–	Ojibwa	to roast until puckered up
Delaware	English name	Oneida	people of the stone
Erie	raccoon nation	Onondaga	people on the hill
Fox	red earth people	Ottawa	to trade
Huron	rough or ruffian	Passamaquoddy	those who pursue the pollock
Illini	people	Paugusset	where the narrows open out
Iroquois	real adders (snakes)	Pennacook	downhill
Kickapoo	he stands about	Pequot	destroyers?
Mahican	wolf (or place name)	Petun	French name
Malecite	broken talkers	Pocomtuc	–
Mascouten	prairie people	Potawatomi	people of the place of fire?
Massachuset	at the range of hills	Powhatan	falls in a current of water
Menomini	wild rice men	Sauk	people of the yellow earth
Miami	people of the Peninsula	Seneca	people of the mountain
Micmac	allies	Shawnee	southerners
Mingo	Delaware term	Stockbridge	English name
Mississauga	river with several outlets	Susquehannock	–
Mohawk	man eaters	Tuscarora	hemp gatherers
Mohegan	wolf (or place name)	Wampanoag	eastern people
Montauk	place name	Wappinger	easterners (possibly)
Nanticoke	tidewater people	Wenro	floating oil
Narraganset	people of the small point	Western Abenaki	easterners
Neutral	English name	Winnebago	people of the filthy water

PORCUPINE QUILLWORK

One of the principal decorative arts of North America involved the use of porcupine quills. The porcupine was found in the northeastern United States, much of the western U.S., and throughout Canada and Alaska. Its southern limit is a matter of debate, as quillwork has been reported as far south as the lower Mississippi valley and among the Cherokees. Quills were softened by water, teeth, or nails, dyed with natural plant color, or—after 1850—by traded commercial aniline dyes or boiled out colors from traded blankets. Quills were applied to buckskin by various techniques, such as wrapping, braiding, and weaving, by Woodland, Plains, and Subarctic tribes. Among the Micmac, Ojibwa, and Ottawa, quills were also attached to birch bark. Beadwork largely replaced quillwork by the 1860s, but quillwork has continued to be practiced in a number of places.

DELAWARE

Below: **Carolina Algonkian warrior, c. 1585. Watercolor sketches made by John White, one of Sir Walter Raleigh's colonists, near the settlement at Roanoke Island in 1585–87, are preserved in the British Museum. He reported that warriors from around present-day Albemarle Sound, North Carolina, decorated their bodies with paint and pearls (probably shells or Roanoke wampum). This warrior, derived from White's drawings, has an animal skin apron and a bow probably of maple or hazel.**

The most important collection of Algonkian groups of the mid-Atlantic coast, the Delaware or Leni-Lenape once occupied the lower Hudson River valley, the western part of Long Island, and the whole of the present state of New Jersey south to Delaware Bay. Their language difference from neighboring peoples is not clear; perhaps even the Wappinger of the Hudson River and the Matinecock of Long Island should really be included in their group. The Delaware group included the Esopus on the west bank of the Hudson; the Rockaway and Canarsee of Long Island; the Minisinks (later called Munsee) on the Delaware River north of the Delaware Water Gap; the Unami, whose dialect was spoken on both sides of the Delaware River in New Jersey and Pennsylvania; the Raritans on the Raritan River; a number of minor subtribes occupying Manhattan Island north to present Westchester County, New York; and a number of small tribes and villages on the lower Delaware below present-day Philadelphia, who also spoke a variation of Unami and can be considered as one. In later years they were usually classified in three groups—Munsee, Unami, and Unalachtigo— but only the former two were true divisions.

The Delaware were probably first seen by Europeans in 1524, when Giovanni da Verrazano sailed into New York harbor, but their history of real contact with Europeans began with Henry Hudson's visit in 1609. By the 1630s, the Dutch had introduced the fur trade. The Delaware fought to secure their villages and hunting territories against the encroaching Dutch and northern Indians. The English who succeeded the Dutch created an alliance called the Covenant Chain with the River Indians, including the Iroquois, Mohican, and Delaware.

Throughout the seventeenth century the Delaware were swept by European diseases to which they had little immunity: smallpox, measles, influenza, and plagues, which halved their population. By the 1740s they were being crowded out by whites and began to move west to the Susquehanna and Allegheny Rivers, fighting at times against English settlers and at times for them against the French. They finally made peace at Easton, New Jersey, in 1758 when a reservation was established for some remaining New Jersey bands at Brotherton. By now the Delaware were strung out in settlements from New Jersey to the Ohio country. The western bands actively engaged in frontier warfare until the Treaty of Greenville (1795), after which some moved west to the White River in Indiana and later to Cape Girardeau, Missouri. A number of other groups in Pennsylvania and Ohio had been converted to Christianity by German Moravians and moved to the Thames River, Ontario. Still others had joined some Mohican and Nanticoke and sought Iroquois protection, moving with them to Ontario after the American Revolution. The Brothertons joined the Stockbridges in New York in 1802 and ultimately moved to Wisconsin with the Oneida in 1833.

During their migration westward, the Delaware maintained a way of life that was more influenced by white ways than those of the less Europeanized Indians of the interior. They replaced their bark longhouses with log cabins; native slash-and-burn farming evolved into European farming with cattle, horses, and swine; bowls, dishes, pestles and

WIGWAM

An oval or conical lodge of the northeastern Algonkians, constructed of birch bark or rush mats fixed to a frame of saplings. The term wigwam applies to several Woodland forms. The four main types were domed, peaked, tipi shaped, and the bark house. The domed wigwam, of ironwood saplings driven into the ground and bent over to form arches, was covered with birch or elm bark or reed mats. The peaked roof lodge had a series of pointed arches connected by a ridgepole, also covered with bark or mats. The tipi shape had a conical frame of poles covered with bark. The bark house was a rectangular structure of poles with bark sheet outer covering. Most of these single-family homes had central smoke holes. Ceremonial lodges were similar to the domed type, but longer and open-ended. Canvas was also sometimes used as a covering. Wigwams were in use in isolated areas until c. 1900; a few are still made for special occasions.

Left: **Delaware wigwam, a reconstructed elm bark lodge and dugout canoe at historic Fort Delaware, a reconstructed traders' fort near Narrowsburg, New York, on the Delaware River.**

Above: **Delaware moccasins made by the Oklahoma traditionalist Nora Thompson Dean, c. 1970. They are buckskin with the Woodland center seam, one-piece construction, and ribbonwork on the flaps.**

mortars, fiber bags, tumplines (straps going around the forehead or chest and used to support a pack on the back), baskets, and mats had been replaced by trade goods. During the nineteenth century, often in concert with the Shawnee, the Delaware moved farther west. By the 1820s they were in southern Missouri and by the 1830s in Kansas, where some settled and became citizens in Ottawa and Franklin Counties. The last major move was in 1867–68 to Oklahoma, where the largest group settled in the Cherokee Nation.

Their earlier population may have been 12,000; today they have about 8,000 descendants, all of mixed white or Mohican ancestry. Approximately 350 are on the Six Nations Reserve in Ontario; 500 on the Moravian Reserve near Bothwell, Ontario; 200 Munsee near Munceytown, Ontario; and several hundred mixed with the Stockbridge and Brotherton in Wisconsin. There are a few Delaware citizens in Kansas; but the largest group are the Registered Delaware of Washington, Nowata, Craig, and Delaware Counties in Oklahoma, numbering about 1,100. A hundred or so descendants of the Delaware who moved to Oklahoma from Texas with the Caddo and Wichita now live near Anadarko, Oklahoma. Only a handful of Munsee or Unami speakers survive today. The Oklahoma Delaware sponsor a Pan-Indian Powwow each summer. A small number never left New Jersey and a few, near Eatontown, claim their Delaware ancestry.

The Delaware, occupying a central homeland among the Atlantic coast Algonkians, held the highest political rank; many other tribes claimed to have diverged from them and accorded them the respectful title of "grandfather." The Nanticoke, Conoy, Shawnee, and Mohican all claimed a connection with them. Their real name, Leni-Lenape, is equivalent to "real men"; but their common English name is derived from Lord de la Warr, an early governor of the colony at Jamestown, Virginia, although he never set foot among the people who have ever since carried his name.

Although the recording of Delaware religion and culture took place long after Christian and other influences may have blurred many details, they seem to have believed in a great Manito, or Creator, whose spiritual agents were present in all of nature: trees, flowers, grass, rocks, and rivers. Their ceremonies were in response to or to control the weather, hunting, or harvest, or for the elimination of sickness and catastrophe. The "Big House" Ceremony was still held among the Oklahoma Delawares until the 1920s. A wooden building (originally bark) was constructed with twelve faces carved on the interior posts to watch the ceremonials and to carry prayers to the Creator. Their creation myth (shared with other eastern tribes) held that the Delaware sprang from a hole in the earth, and that the world was carried on a giant turtle's back. During the nineteenth century, a certain Dr. Brinton reproduced a series of 183 mnemonic glyphs (symbolic writing intended to aid the memory) which he claimed were a record of ancient Delaware history and myths called the Walam Olum, or "red score." The originals have not survived, and some historians believe Brinton's records and his sources are questionable.

No tribe was pushed so far from its homelands as the Delaware. A few bands during the nineteenth century even became "mountain men" in the Far West, and many claimed they were better military auxiliaries than the Pawnee or Cheyenne. They also mixed their bloodlines with several tribes in the West, notably the Flathead and Nez Perce.

CENSUS 2000

Delaware	5,555
Delaware Tribe of Indians, Oklahoma	102
Lenni-Lanape	1,558
Munsee	124
Delaware Tribe of Western Oklahoma	131
Ramapough Mountain	719
Sand Hill Band of Delaware Indians	6
Total	8,304

Below: **Delaware or Iroquois headdress and skin coat, c. 1850.**

HURON (WYANDOT)

Below: **Huron of Lorette chief, c. 1840. The refugee Huron group that settled near Quebec City gradually adopted French cultural traits but retained many of their traditional crafts. Moosehair embroidery and quillwork, used to decorate souvenir trade items, also appeared on the cuffs, shoulders, and collars of men's dress clothes. He wears a French Canadian–made assumption sash, probably derived from and replacing the native-made finger-woven sash of fiber or traded woolen yarn.**

An Iroquoian people who lived north and west of Lake Simcoe in present-day Ontario, between Nottawassaga and Matchedash Bays, and were first contacted during the early seventeenth century by the French, who established missions among them. The Jesuit missions recorded much of their culture at that time and reported a sizable population of 30,000 in over thirty villages of longhouses, some defended by fortifications, but most open and defenseless. They were slash-and-burn agriculturalists who gathered fruits, hunted, fished, and actively traded fur, especially beaver, with the French. They often warred with the Seneca, and in 1648–49 the Five Nations invaded their lands in present-day Ontario in pursuit of expansion and control of the fur trade. Huronia was abandoned; a large number of Hurons were taken in by the Iroquois or fled west, although a few found refuge at Lorette near Quebec City. The Lorette Hurons modified their culture with strong French-Canadian influences over the years and have frequently married Canadians.

Huron (and some Petun) who moved west seem to have gone first to Mackinac, Michigan and then to Green Bay, Wisconsin, but ultimately to the Detroit, Michigan, area and the Sandusky River region of northern Ohio by the early eighteenth century. Here the British knew them as Wyandot, and they were often involved in the colonial conflicts of the area. For those in the Detroit area, a reserve was established in the Anderdon township, Essex County, Ontario, in 1790, but later ceded to the British Crown, although a few people of mixed descent survived in the area until the twentieth century.

By 1817, the Wyandots in Ohio retained only two small reservations, which were later sold. During the 1840s they removed first to Kansas and, after 1853, to northeastern Indian Territory, now Oklahoma. Throughout their later history they frequently mixed with Euro-Americans and were often divided among themselves between Christians and those who practiced traditional religion. A number (about 300) became U.S. citizens while in Kansas and never removed to Oklahoma.

By 1961 about 900 Wyandot descendants were recorded at the old Quapaw Agency in Ottawa County, Oklahoma, although only a portion lived on their old lands and just two elderly native speakers were left. A few remained in Wyandot County, Kansas, while 1,041 were counted in Lorette, Quebec, in 1969. The latter group were for many years noted for their fine craftwork sold to collectors. Census 2000 gave the current Wyandot figure as 1,850–3,531, including those with part-parentage. They are a federally recognized tribe.

Above: **Card case of made of two layers of bark and embroidered with dyed moose hair in floral designs. Probably made in about 1850.**

Below: **Mary Kelley, Wyandot, Oklahoma, c. 1912.**

HURON MOCCASINS

The true moccasin forms with soft soles (made without left or right feet) were made and decorated in a wide variety of ways, but there seem to be two main subtypes. One is a southern tradition made with a front-seam moccasin, the other a northern

the nineteenth century imported it to replace the center-front seam construction. This vamp form, however, was always present in the far North, reaching back to Siberia. Its later adoption in the eastern parts of North America may have been due to the influence of the fur trade and links with the St. Lawrence River and the far North trading companies in the commerce of the eighteenth and nineteenth centuries.

Most of the Huron moccasins that survive in museums are attributed to the Huron village of Lorette in Quebec. These are sometimes beautifully decorated with moose hair and caribou hair embroidery. The transitional Huron moccasin, c. 1840–1860, had a deep, long, or narrow vamp with the cuffs or flaps turned down. The earliest forms usually had the flaps upright to the leg and occasionally both an upright flap and a cuff. Some of the

early moccasins of the eastern Great Lakes area were characteristically dyed black. Huron moccasins, together with moccasins of the Têtes de Boule (French for "round heads," a branch of the Cree), were sold in large numbers by the Hudson's Bay Company, and this may have been a factor in the spread of the numerous construction variations and decoration techniques across Canada.

tradition with a vamp or apron at the instep. There are many variations on these subtypes, as well as hybrids of both forms. Some have imagined a European origin for the vamp, as numerous tribes during

Top, Above, and Left: **Huron moccasins.**

Above left: **Huron of Lorette moccasins of black dyed buckskin with moosehair embroidery decoration, c. 1820.**

A confederacy of five, later six, Iroquoian tribes living in the central northern area of present upper New York State. Their league united formerly warring nations in order to preserve the integrity of each and also bound them to a common council with a fixed number of *Sachems* or chiefs from each tribe—fifty for the whole confederacy. Dekanawida and the historical Hiawatha are traditionally reported to have founded the confederacy between A.D. 900 and A.D.1500. Their Great Law of Peace continues today as one of the oldest forms of democracy, with lineage, clan, and tribe represented in policy- making. The Sachems are nominated by eligible clan mothers. The league originally included the Mohawk (see pages 30–31), Oneida (see page 23), Onondaga (see pages 38–39), Cayuga (see page 22), and Seneca (see page 24), living in this order from east to west across present central New York State.

They became frequent and bitter enemies of the French but were friendly to Dutch and English traders working out of Albany, New York. During the seventeenth century they launched a series of devastating attacks on related Iroquois-speaking tribes who were under French influence and thus established their supremacy in the beaver fur trade for a century or more. They were important allies of the British during the French and Indian War (1754–63), but the American Revolution (1775–83) broke them. Mohawks, Cayugas, and some Senecas fought with the British, while Oneidas fought alongside the Americans. The Americans had laid waste to much of Iroquoia by the end of the war. The Mohawk and Cayuga mainly withdrew to Canada, the Onondaga and Seneca remained in New York; the Oneida, in time, moved to Wisconsin.

Culturally the Iroquois are believed to be descendants of the prehistoric Mississippian culture. Living in semi-permanent villages, they raised adjacent fields of corn (maize), beans, and squash,

Above: **Iroquois, c. 1812. These northeastern Woodland people had already used European-made tomahawks, guns, cloth, and silver for more than a century. Use of the bow was by now rare in many areas, restricted to some hunting or circumstances when firearms were in short supply. Woodland bows, often of hickory or hazel with braided sinew strings, could exceed 6 feet (2 meters) in length; arrows were sometimes of elder, quivers of bark or rush. The buckskin cap is decorated with traded feathers, cut feather clusters, and ermine skins.**

which supplemented their hunting and gathering. Their entire process of planting, cultivating, harvesting, and food preparation was in the hands of women, whose leaders were called "Matrons." The ceremonial spirits of maize, beans, and squash were called the "Three Sisters." Their religion was dualistic and dedicated to pleasing the spirits, both friendly and unfriendly. The Iroquois seem to have believed in a Creator, at least in later ceremonial practices, and in orenda, the natural power of creativity in all things. As the fur trade and farming became the principal lifestyle of Iroquois communities, healing practices became important in Iroquois religious life, with the appearance of medicine societies such as the

Above: **Iroquois, c. 1880. Woman pounding corn with pestle and log mortar, her child hanging safely nearby. The cradle was a board about 2 feet (0.5 m) long, with a projecting bow similar to those of the Ojibwa but lacking their distinctive recurve; the bow and top edge of the board were often carved and near the bottom was a foot support. The baby was bound to the board with red or blue cloth decorated with beads or moose hair, and a blanket or netting could be drawn over the bow to protect the face. A strap secured the cradle behind the mother's shoulders.**

Right: **Iroquois couple pounding corn with pestle and mortar, probably photographed on the Six Nations Reserve, Ontario, c. 1890. The split log house is typical of the adaptation to white rural life; one of the baskets appears to be of the native splint ash type.**

20

FALSE FACES

Northeastern Woodland attire worn by Iroquois ceremonialists, c. 1840. Two male societies performed at several of the annual festivals in the agricultural calendar. Their Corn Husk Faces heralded the Maize, Bean, and Squash deities—the life-supporting "Three Sisters." They wore misshapen wooden masks to represent the False Faces, with which they exorcised (drove out by means of ritual) illness and evil during the Midwinter Festival.

Above: **Indian Chief of Six Nations (Iroquois) c. 1860s,** photographer unknown. The man wears a beaded cap with feathers and horsehair. He also wears a beaded baldric over a buckskin jacket.

False Faces, a mask-wearing society devoted to group well-being and healing processes.

At the end of the eighteenth century (a time of despair for many Iroquois communities as white culture and law continued to encroach on their way of life), a Seneca holy man named Handsome Lake revitalized Iroquois religion by introducing a strict moral code to a modified ceremonial life, partly influenced by American Quakers. This "Longhouse" religion still survives in twelve Iroquois communities today, preserving the remnants of Iroquois culture, language, ritual, and drama for a small percentage of their descendants. The term "Longhouse" derives from their ancient bark dwelling, which housed several families. From the time of the American Revolution, Iroquois have gradually made a transition to a Euro-American culture and have for many generations lived similarly to rural whites (or more recently as wage-earners), with a large number living in towns and cities away from their reserves and communities. Their population by 1980 exceeded 50,000 descendants, including a large number of persons of mixed European and other tribal ancestry added over four centuries of expansion, conflict, and acculturation.

CAYUGA

A tribe of the Iroquoian family and of the Iroquois Confederation, formerly occupying the shores of Cayuga Lake in present New York State. Their local council was composed of four kinship groups, and according to tradition, this form shaped the pattern of the confederation of the Five (later Six) Nations, in which the Cayuga had ten delegates. In 1660, they were estimated to number 1,500 and in 1778 about 1,100. At the beginning of the American Revolution, a large part of the tribe removed to Canada and never returned, while the rest were scattered among other tribes of the Iroquois League. In 1795 they ceded their lands to New York State without federal approval; some joined the Seneca of Sandusky in Ohio; others joined the Oneida who later moved to Wisconsin. The mixed Seneca-Cayuga ultimately found their way to Oklahoma.

Today, many Cayugas are mixed with other Iroquois people and also with whites; the largest group in New York State live on their Cattaraugus Reservation. The largest number, however, live on the Six Nations Reserve on the Grand River, Ontario, Canada, where 1,450 were reported in 1955; the same group was reported to number 2,525 in 1973.

Today, two Cayuga Longhouse congregations still number several hundred on the Grand River and continue the traditional ceremonials organized by the Seneca revivalist Handsome Lake at the close of the eighteenth century. Another Longhouse group survives among the Seneca-Cayuga of Oklahoma. In 2000, the Cayuga settled the largest Indian land claim in U.S. history, almost a quarter of a billion dollars, because the type of treaty by which New York acquired their land is specifically forbidden in the U.S. Constitution.

ONEIDA

"People of the stone," refering to the Oneida stone, a granite boulder near their former village: a tribe of Iroquoian stock forming one of the Six Nations of the Iroquois League. They lived around Oneida Lake and in the region southward to the Susquehanna River. Not loyal to the league's policy of friendliness towards the British, they preferred the French and were practically the only tribe to fight for the Americans in the War of Independence. Attacked by Joseph Brant's Mohawks during that war, they were forced to take refuge in American settlements until the war ended. Factionalism and a reduction of their land base in New York State persuaded many Oneida to move to Wisconsin, where the Menomini gave up land for their use in 1838. Another group purchased 5,200 acres (2,100 hectares) near London, Ontario in the 1840s, independently from the Oneidas already at Six Nations. A few remained in New York State near their old homes or on the Onondaga Reserve.

In 1926, some 3,238 Oneidas remained in the United States, 2,976 on or near their Green Bay Reservation, Wisconsin, and 262 in New York State. In 1972, the Oneida of the Thames near London, Ontario, included 1,964 members, of

IROQUOIAN
One of the most important linguistic families of the Eastern Woodlands, consisting of a northern branch originally occupying the St. Lawrence valley from Montreal to Ile d'Orleans plus the Huron, Petun, and Neutral of present southern Ontario; the Five Nations of New York State; also the Susquehannock of Pennsylvania; a southern branch in Virginia and North Carolina comprising the Nottoway, Meherrin, and Tuscarora; and finally, a divergent southern branch, the Cherokee. The Iroquoians were once proposed to be distantly related to the Caddoans of the southern Plains, which fitted their assumed southern origins; but both propositions were subsequently discredited, since they seem to have been a northern people as far back as 1000 B.C.

Below: **Iroquois glengarry hat, decorated with beadwork, c. 1870, a direct adaptation of Scottish Highlanders' headgear.**

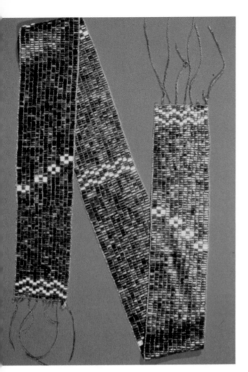

Above: **Wampum belt, Iroquois, c. 1770. Originally these belts were of native drilled tubular shell beads, later of trade glass beads in imitation. These belts were woven to solemnize and record treaties and important events.**

CENSUS 2000 (U.S.)

The numbers recorded for the Iroquois were:

Cayuga Nation	964
Iroquois	3,157
Mohawk	13,940
Oneida Nation of New York	11,057
Onondaga	2,130
Seneca	7,203
Seneca Nation	614
Seneca-Cayuga	1,509
Tonawanda Band of Seneca	266
Tuscarora	2,308
Wyandotte	1,850
Total	45,212

whom 1,200 were residing on the reserve lands; and 802 Oneidas by lineage were reported from Six Nation Reserve, Brantford, Ontario, in 1973. A few hundred were mixed together with several Iroquois groups in New York, chiefly at the Onondaga Reservation or near the Oneida settlement. The Wisconsin Oneida had over 6,000 members, but only 2,000 residents on or near tribal lands near Green Bay in 1972. Census 2000 reported the Oneida Tribe of Wisconsin as 920 (including part Oneida). Most Oneidas became Christians before leaving New York, although a Longhouse minority survives at the Thames Band Reserve near London, Ontario.

SENECA

They called themselves "people of the mountain" and were once the most populous tribe of the Iroquois Confederacy, with a range in western New York State between the Genesse River and Seneca Lake. They became the most important tribe of the confederacy, and on the defeat of the Erie and Neutral tribes they occupied the country near Lake Erie and south along the Allegheny Mountains. Consistently friendly towards the British, the Seneca fought for them in the French and Indian War and later in the American War of Independence, although some remained neutral. General John Sullivan destroyed Seneca villages and crops in 1779, and many fled to British protection. The last time the Seneca aided others in war was in 1812 during the U.S. invasion of British Canada.

Instead of receding before the Europeans' rapidly increasing population as it pressed upon their remaining lands in New York, the Seneca tenaciously maintained their ground, and when forced to make territorial concessions to the whites they managed to preserve a few tracts for their own use, which they continue to occupy. The present Seneca descendants are on three reservations in western New York at Allegany and Cattaraugus (the Seneca Republic), plus Tonawanda near Akron. Their small Cornplanter tract in Pennsylvania was flooded by the Kinzua Dam in the 1960s. In 1890 these groups numbered about 3,000; in 1906, 2,742; in 1956, 3,528; and in 1970, 4,644. There are also several hundred Senecas among the descendants of the mixed Seneca-Cayuga of Oklahoma, and 345 Seneca were reported from Six Nations, Ontario, in 1973. Each Seneca reservation has a Longhouse congregation, and the Allegany Senecas run the Seneca-Iroquois National Museum at Salamanca, New York. (For 2000 U.S. Census figures, see the chart on page 24.)

TUSCARORA

An Iroquoian tribe originally of present North Carolina, who divided from their northern kinsmen perhaps 600 years ago. They lived along the Pamlico, Neuse, and Trent rivers in northeastern North Carolina in the Piedmont and coastal plain. Their final defeat by white settlers in 1711–13, following years of persecution and usurpation of their lands in the Carolinas, resulted in their move north to join the Iroquois League of New York State as a sixth nation. They were formally adopted in 1722; nevertheless, there was a Tuscarora Indian band in Bertie County, North Carolina, later during the 18th century, and the last of them did not move north until 1803. During the Revolution part of them moved to British Canada, where their descendants are among the Iroquois of the Six Nations Reserve on the Grand River near Brantford; others remained in New York State on a reservation which bears their name near Niagara Falls. In the War of 1812 some Tuscaroras performed meritorious service for the Americans. The tribe has been one of the most acculturated of the New York Iroquois groups, abandoning Native culture in favor of Christianity (Baptist), shown by their lack of northern Iroquoian mask-making and revised Longhouse religion associated with other Iroquois groups. Not all of those with Tuscarora ancestry moved north: some may have joined the modern Person County Indians and Lumbees of North Carolina. In their North Carolina days, they perhaps numbered 5,000. In 1890, 400 Tuscaroras lived on their New York Reservation, and about 700 in 1970; Grand River numbered 789 in 1973. (See the chart on page 24 for 2000 Census.)

NORTHEASTERN PURSES
Purses seem to have had a particular fascination for white visitors to the northeastern states, many of them souvenir collectors. Niagara Falls was a major center for Indian crafts from as far away as the Maritime provinces of Canada, and quill- and hair-embroidered bark, split-wood baskets, and beaded items found a ready market. The Iroquois were the principal Native group involved in the trade. The Tuscaroras and Mohawks from Brantford, Ontario, lived very close to Niagara and were no doubt major producers of beaded material. However, the Mohawk of Caughnawaga and the Allegany-Seneca among the Iroquois, and the Micmac, Malecite, St. Francis Abenaki, Penobscot, Passamaquoddy, and remnant Algonkians of New England, plus the Eastern Ojibwa, all added material to the pool of souvenir crafts. Indian purses were usually constructed on a background of wool flannel, red or blue, or sometimes velvet of purple, yellow, blue, black, even green color, backed by a loosely woven cotton fabric or taffeta. Some of the older purses have beaded designs that clearly incorporate early Indian design motifs.

MAHICAN (MOHICAN)

STOCKBRIDGE

The name given to a group of Mahican, Wappinger, Housatonic, and other Indians originally settled at Schaghticoke, New York, who subsequently gathered at the town and mission of Stockbridge, Massachusetts, in 1736. They supported the British in the French and Indian War and the Americans in the Revolution. Between 1756 and 1785 they joined other groups, at first in Broome and Tioga counties, New York, and later joined the Oneida along with the Brotherton refugees. The Oneida, Stockbridge, and Brotherton all moved to Wisconsin in 1833. The Stockbridge were given a separate reservation southwest of the Menominee near Bowler, Wisconsin. In 1966, 380 "Stockbridge-Munsee" were still living on the reservation, with an equal number living away. By Census 2000, the figures were: Stockbridge-Munsee Community of Mohican Indians of Wisconsin 2,012 (1,565 part).

An important Algonkian people of the Hudson River valley in New York from Lake George south to the Catskill Mountains. The Mahican or Mohican are often confused with another, separate tribe of Connecticut, the Mohegan. Both may have been the inspiration of James Fenimore Cooper's *The Last of the Mohicans*, but both peoples still survive. The Wappinger (proper), Housatonic River groups, and Esopus are sometimes classed with this group. The Mahicans lived in palisaded villages, bark longhouses, and wigwams; they grew corn, fished, gathered, and hunted. In August the men returned to their villages for the Green Corn ceremonials and to assist the women in the harvest. They carved wood and bark vessels, wooden spoons and dishes, but had no pottery. They made canoes, wore skin clothing, and traded wampum to the tribes farther north. Their first contacts with Europeans came in 1609 when Henry Hudson sailed up the Hudson River, and, with the establishment of Fort Orange and Albany by the Dutch, they were quickly drawn into the fur trade.

From the 1720s on, the Mahicans began to move west to the Susquehanna River and then to the Ohio country. The rest resettled at Stockbridge, Massachusetts, with the Housatonic in 1736; then after 1756 moved to New York; and finally in 1833 to Wisconsin, where the combined Mahican-Wappinger-Housatonic, now called "Stockbridge," obtained a reservation near Bowler, Shawano County. Several hundred people of mixed Stockbridge and Munsee descent remain there. A few Mohicans remained in the Hudson Valley.

A small group of Algonkians located along the St. John River in what is now New Brunswick, Canada. The Malecite (or Maliseet) are closely related to, if not originally the same people as, the Passamaquoddy of Maine and are related more distantly to the Micmac, Penobscot, and Abenaki, the four sometimes known as "Wabanaki." The Malecite were also known as Etchemin, a term also applied to their relatives. First recorded by the French explorer Samuel de Champlain, they were thereafter under French influence until the British conquest of Canada. Subsequently they lost most of their lands except for a few acres on the St. John and Tobique Rivers, where a number of Malecite descendants still remain, now of mixed Indian-European ancestry from four hundred years of white contact. Their Native culture was overwhelmed generations ago, and the tribe largely converted to Roman Catholicism. The Malecite were noted during the nineteenth century for excellent beadwork, which survives in several museum collections. Their population was rarely given as more than a few hundred; perhaps 2,000 descendants are still found at their reserves at Woodstock and Tobique in New Brunswick and Viger, Quebec, and a few others in Maine around Presque Isle and Houlton, Aroostook County, with some Micmac. The Houlton Malecite numbered 550 members in 1990. Census 2000 provided the following figures: Malecite 1,288 (including 416 part Malecite); Houlton Band of Maliseet Indians 33.

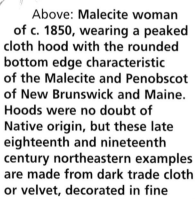

Above: **Malecite woman of c. 1850, wearing a peaked cloth hood with the rounded bottom edge characteristic of the Malecite and Penobscot of New Brunswick and Maine. Hoods were no doubt of Native origin, but these late eighteenth and nineteenth century northeastern examples are made from dark trade cloth or velvet, decorated in fine floralistic double-curve and zigzag beaded designs; by this date they were worn only for galas or church festivals.**

Left: **Three Malecite beaded cloth pouches and a sash—perhaps a priest's stole—decorated with delicate beadwork of the style of the mid-nineteenth century.**

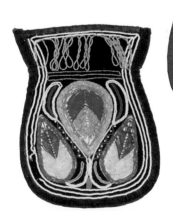

An important Algonkian people of Maritime Canada who lived in Nova Scotia, Cape Breton Island, Prince Edward Island, and in fairly recent times parts of southern Newfoundland. Micmacs were among the first Native people encountered by Europeans on the North American continent. The explorer John Cabot took three Micmac Natives back to England with him in 1497. Afterward they were constantly visited by explorers and fishing vessels from France and England, and became intermediaries in trade between the French on the St. Lawrence River and tribes farther south. Consequently they became allies of the French, aiding them in colonial conflicts with the English even after what is now Nova Scotia (then called Acadia) had been ceded to Great Britain by treaty. Since 1779 the Micmac have been peaceful, living scattered across their former domain. Unlike many other Northeast tribes, they were never deported to the south; but a long association with whites, particularly the French, has caused a gradual loss of their traditional culture and traditions and the inevitable mixing of ancestry. Over the years they have been noted for the fine decoration of birch bark

Above: **Nova Scotia Micmac woman, c. 1840. The ancient, double-curve motif in a series of laterally repeated designs probably represents canoes. The symbol was used on clothing, pouches, bark containers, and canoes by most northeastern Algonkian peoples, and occurs as far west as the Blackfoot range (in present-day Montana and Alberta).**

Right: **Micmac Indians in front of a makeshift wigwam, Nova Scotia, c. 1900. They are making splint-ash baskets by plaiting strips of wood, a type of craft made throughout the Northeast by Algonkians and Iroquois. Sometimes the splints were stamped with potato-cut designs or dyed. Some baskets were reinforced on the edge with sweet grass.**

souvenirs with porcupine quillwork and the production of split wood basketry, both of which have been sold to generations of white curio hunters.

Their numbers have usually been reported as about 5,000 in early times, and while their present numbers of over 15,000 includes a large proportion of people of mixed Indian-European descent, over 9,800 Micmac are found scattered on about thirty reserves and communities, the largest at Restigouche, Quebec (1,400); Eskasoni on Cape Breton Island (1,300); Shubenacadie, Nova Scotia (900); and Burnt Church and Big Cove, New Brunswick (1,600). The Micmacs' Native Algonkian language is still spoken by several hundred people, but Catholicism has replaced most Native religious beliefs for many generations. U.S. Micmac numbers reported in the 2000 census are 6,722 (including part Micmac).

In ancient times, the Micmac hunted caribou, moose, otter, and beaver and also fished and gathered shellfish. Their dwellings were usually conical bark wigwams; transportation was by distinctively shaped bark canoes. Native dress made from animal hides seems to have been replaced quickly by dark cloth obtained from European traders, which the Micmac often decorated with beads and ribbons. They were sometimes also known as Tarrantine.

Above: **Micmac man's ceremonial costume, c. 1825. The coat is European military style in broadcloth with epaulette-like decorations on the shoulders and cuffs with double curve motif beadwork in white beads. The leggings are of red cloth and similarly beaded.**

Left: **Assorted Micmac birch bark items, including the distinctively shaped canoe, decorated with quillwork.**

Above: **A northeastern woman in a photograph taken in the early years of the twentieth century, making split basketry.**

The easternmost tribe of the Iroquois League, who once lived mainly in the valley of the Mohawk River in present east-central New York State. The Mohawk were the "keepers of the eastern door" of the Iroquois confederacy. With the encouragement of the Dutch traders at Albany, they became one of the most aggressive peoples of the area and were probably responsible for the depletion of some of the tribes on their borders. During the seventeenth century they were firm friends of the Dutch and British. The French explorer-soldier Samuel de Champlain had attacked their settlements, and henceforth they were enemies of the French. This lasted until between 1667 and 1720. At that time, during breaks in the conflicts between France and Britain, more than a third of the Mohawks withdrew to French Canada under Jesuit missionary influence.

The Mohawks remaining in New York continued to support the British during the French and Indian War; and gave considerable assistance to them during the American Revolution under Joseph Brant (Thayendanegea), an Anglicized Mohawk leader. At the end of the war the pro-British Mohawks took refuge in Canada with a large party of British Loyalists and obtained a tract of land on the Grand River along with groups of other Iroquois until all six Iroquois tribes were represented (the Tuscarora having joined as a sixth nation). In 1784, another Mohawk group established a settlement near Kingston, Ontario, known as the Tyendinaga Band. A few subsequently left for the West as fur trappers and finally settled in Alberta; a few others went to Gibson and Watha near Georgina Bay, Ontario.

The history of the French Mohawks developed quite separately. During the latter part of the seventeenth century they went first to La Prairie, where they were joined by some Onondagas and Algonkians. Subsequently they formed New York settlements at Oka (Lake of Two Mountains); later they founded Caughnawaga (Kahawake) and St.

Regis (Akwesasne). They usually assisted the French in colonial conflicts. All these groups have survived until today as reserve bands, and the Mohawk population consists of the following groups: Oka, on the north side of the St. Lawrence, in Quebec—1907 population 507, in 1970, 777; Caughnawaga, on the south side of the St. Lawrence—3,198 reported in 1949 and 4,515 in 1970; St. Regis, on the U.S. border partly in Quebec, Ontario, and New York—1,800 reported in 1945 on the U.S. side, 1,100 in Quebec, and 600 in Ontario in 1949. In 1970, 2,963 Mohawk were living on the Canadian side.

At Tyendinaga at Bay of Quinte, Ontario, 2,111 were reported in 1970, and in the same year at Six Nations Reserve on the Grand River, Ontario, 3,974 were reported as Mohawk by descent. A few are at Gibson and Watha on Parry Sound, Georgina Bay, Ontario, with the total given as 206 in 1970; and a few (called Michel's band) in Alberta, descendants of fur traders, numbered 125 of mixed descent in 1949.

The Census 2000 figures give a present population of 26,851, although largely of mixed ancestry—only 13,940 are single-tribe respondents. The Mohawk are noted for having accepted the various forms of Christianity, although a Longhouse is now thriving on the St. Regis-Akwesasne Reservation among a largely Catholic population. Their men have also been noted in recent times for working as highly skilled steel workers on high-rise buildings and bridges throughout the United States and Canada. Recently, several families from Akwesasne have established another community at Ganienkeh near the northern end of Lake Champlain in Quebec and also near their old homes in the Mohawk Valley near Fonda, New York.

Tribal names are—for the most part—not the old names the Indians knew themselves. Many names translate simply as the "real men" or "original people." The common, popular, modern names used are derived from various sources. Some are from Native terms, either from the people themselves or names applied by neighbors or enemies, or corruptions of these terms. Some tribal names are anglicized (made English) forms of translated Native names; others are from French or Spanish sources. We use the tribal names most commonly encountered in history and literature, although it should be noted that some modern Indian groups have successfully reintroduced their own names into current usage.

Below: **Northeastern quilled moccasins.**

OJIBWA (CHIPPEWA)

Right: **Ojibwa men on Red Lake Reservation, northern Minnesota, c. 1900. Several wear heavily beaded bandolier pouches; the floral patterns are thought to have developed through a combination of European folk art with Native curvilinear (using curved lines) decorative traditions.**

Below: **Northeastern Algonkian ceremonial hooded cape—see caption on page 2.**

One of the largest tribes of North America and the principal one of the Algonkian language family. The Ojibwa original home was Sault Sainte Marie, Ontario. They were first mentioned by the French explorer Jean Nicolet in 1640, along with other local groups who were probably related to them. They became deeply involved in the fur trade from about 1670 and in the course of the 18th century spread both east (to be called Missisauga) and northwest (Saulteaux), even to the northern edge of the Plains (Bungi). Their range was exceeded only by that of the Cree, and their descendant population today is exceeded only by that of the Navajo. The Chippewa or Southern Ojibwa spread into the Upper Michigan Peninsula, Wisconsin, Minnesota, and the Lake of the Woods area of southwestern Ontario during the early years of the fur trade in the late seventeenth century in small, widely scattered, autonomous bands. These groups were not a tribe in a political sense; only in terms of language and some aspects of a commonly shared culture were they one people. Some bands of the Missisaugas and Southern Ojibwa seem to have forged an alliance with the Potawatomi and Ottawa, once designated the "Three Fires," who joined Pontiac's rebellion (1763); but their main energy was directed against the Dakota (Sioux) of central Minnesota, from whom they acquired rich areas of wild rice production.

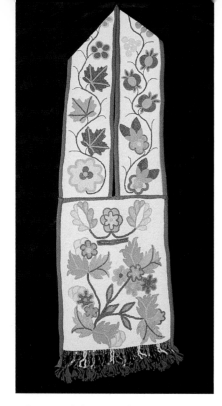

Above: **Elaborate floral beadwork decorates an Ojibwa bandolier bag.**

Far right: **Eastern Ojibwa woman photographed at Muncey Town, Thames River, Ontario, in 1907. Three small groups of Ojibwa, Muncey-Delaware, and Oneida-Iroquois have reserves south of London, Ontario. Although probably Ojibwa (Chippewa), this woman wears a characteristically Iroquoian cloth dress, cape, skirt, and pouch. The same pouch also figures in a contemporary photograph of the Oneida chief John Danford.**

Right: **Model birch bark canoe decorated with porcupine quillwork, with warrior figure and paddle, c. 1850; probably Eastern Ojibwa.**

The land of the Ojibwa was connected by a vast network of interlocking waterways, rivers, and lakes with small portages, which allowed relatively swift forest travel in their light birch bark canoes, refined to the most efficient design. Their technology reflected their forest environment: They carved wooden bowls, ladles, bows, arrows, snowshoes, lacrosse racquets, musical instruments, cradleboards, and fish lures. They used birch bark to cover their wigwams of various shapes and to make containers for carrying, storing, and cooking. They replaced buckskin clothing with cloth obtained from the white traders, and its decoration for festive occasions featured the beads, ribbons, and silver that the Ojibwa developed to replace quillwork and painting. During the nineteenth century they developed two distinctive styles of beadwork: They derived one from earlier decorative forms using large areas of woven beadwork in geometrical forms; the other, more floral in decoration, they sewed onto black or blue broadcloth. This second style may have been influenced by French Canadians, with whom the Ojibwa mixed freely, or by the designs of other immigrant Europeans. The Ojibwa also continued to create porcupine quillwork, but over time this was confined largely to items for the souvenir markets. Their involvement in the fur trade gradually changed Native technology: They replaced their wigwams with log cabins, and guns, knives, kettles, and steel traps replaced earlier indigenous tools and weapons.

Social organization was simple, based on family, bands, and totemic clans named after an animal or bird. In these clans, descent was usually through the father (patrilineal), and members might marry outside the clan. Ojibwa religious beliefs centered on the cosmic force that inhabits trees, rocks,

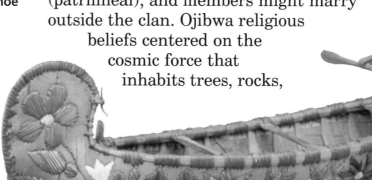

34

sky, earth, and all living things. Presiding over all was a paramount spirit, Manito, perhaps personalized as a result of European influences. The Midewiwin or Grand Medicine Lodge of their Mide religion was an important healing society with membership by payment, a feature of which was the shooting of the sacred shell into the candidate's body and subsequent restoration by the Mide priest. In later years the Ojibwa began practicing the Dream Dance or Drum religion, an early offshoot of the Plains Grass Dance to which they added religious features.

The Ojibwa began to lose their lands by a succession of treaties after the War of 1812, although they were never transported to areas outside their original domain (except for a small group of Swan Creek and Black River Chippewa, who sold their lands in Michigan in 1836 and moved to join the Munsee in Franklin County, Kansas). They were gradually restricted to reservations in the northern parts of the Great Lakes states. As game depleted and the fur trade declined in this region, many gained employment in the logging industry; but the reservations were far from urban centers and thus lacked employment opportunities. Consequently, the Ojibwa living on reservations often suffered from neglect, social problems, poor housing, poor health, and low income.

The loss of more reservation land as a result of the Allotment Act in the 1880s also undermined their land base. In recent times, however, more Ojibwa have moved to urban centers, with perhaps 20,000 people of Ojibwa/Chippewa descent now living in major cities. Native organizations have now taken over more administration and control of their own affairs, initiating new social programs. The population of

CENSUS 2000 (U.S.)

The numbers recorded for the Chippewa were:

Bad River Band of the Lake Superior Tribe	2,686
Bay Mills Indian Community of the Sault Ste. Marie Band	891
Bois Forte/Nett Lake Band of Chippewa	1,175
Burt Lake Chippewa	13
Chippewa	40,557
Fond du Lac	1,483
Grand Portage	4222
Grand Traverse Band of Ottawa and Chippewa Indians	2,615
Keweenaw Bay Indian Community of the L'Anse and Ontonagon Bands	1,130
Lac Courte Oreilles Band of Lake Superior Chippewa	3,210
Lac du Flambeau	1,491
Lac Vieux Desert Band of Lake Superior Chippewa	199
Lake Superior	312
Leech Lake	4,414
Little Shell Chippewa	977
Mille Lacs	2,121
Minnesota Chippewa	2,225
Red Cliff Band of Lake Superior Chippewa	1,609
Red Lake Band of Chippewa	7,525
Saginaw Chippewa	2,186
St. Croix Chippewa	1,008
Sault Ste. Marie Chippewa	8,089
Sokoagon Chippewa	462
Turtle Mountain Band	13,104
White Earth	5,763
Swan Creek Black River Confederate Tribe	51
Total	105,907

the Ojibwa (Chippewa) in the United States was given in 1970 as 41,946, with 50,431 in Canada (including Saulteaux and Missisauga). This figure would be greater, however, if nontreaty Indians were added in Canada. In 1993, almost 80,000 were reported in the United States alone. This population is largely of mixed descent, both from early contacts and affiliation with French trappers and more recent intermarriage with non-Indians.

The Chippewa reservations in the United States are as follows: Michigan—Isabella, Beaver Island, Hog Island, Ontonagon, L'Anse, Bay Mills, plus a number of nonreservation communities; Wisconsin—Lac Courte Oreilles, Lac du Flambeau, Mole Lake, Lac Vieux Desert, Bad River, Red Cliff, and St. Croix lands; Minnesota—Grand Portage, Deer Creek, Leech Lake, Mille Lacs, Vermillion Lake, Nett Lake, Fond du Lac, Red Lake, and White Earth. Reserves in Ontario, Canada, include Pikangikum, Islington, Shoal Lake, The Dalles, English River, Wabauskang, Lac Seul, Eagle Lake, Wabigoon, Rat Portage, Northwest Angle, Big Island, Whitefish Bay, Sabaskong Bay, Big Grassy, Manitou Rapids, Rainy Lake, Sturgeon Falls, Nequagon Lake, and Seine River.

A number of reservations hold summer powwows in which they present a variety of Indian dances (including non-Ojibwa dances). Wild rice is still collected in a few places, as it was in former times; but the spoken language and Mide religion survive only among older Ojibwa people or on remote Canadian reserves. Nevertheless, the Ojibwa/Chippewa are still one of the most important American Indian peoples.

Above: **Ojibwa (Chippewa), floral beaded knife sheath, c. 1890.**

Above Left: **Little Shell, Ojibwa (Chippewa), wearing a treaty, or Peace, medal and a cloth neckband with traditional floral beadwork. The photograph was probably taken during a visit to Washington, D.C., in about 1880.**

Above Right: **Ojibwa (Chippewa) chief Mah-we-do-ke-shick (Spirit of the Skies), c. 1860s. He wears a Hudson's Bay trade blanket and holds a catlinite pipe bowl.**

Left: **This cradleboard and cloth cover are decorated with beadwork, with dentalium shells and other beads attached to the bow to amuse the child. Probably of Swampy (West Main Cree) or Northern Ojibwa creation, early nineteenth century.**

Above: **Onondaga or Micmac pouch.**

An important tribe of the Iroquois Confederacy, formerly living on the mountain, lake, and creek bearing their name in present Onondaga County, New York, extending northward to Lake Ontario and southward perhaps to the headwaters of the Susquehanna River. In the Iroquois Councils the Onondaga are known as "they (who) are the bearers." Their principal village, also the capital of the Confederacy, was called Onondaga, later Onondaga Castle; it was situated from before 1654 to 1681 on Indian Hill in the present town of Pompey, New York, south of modern Syracuse, and in 1677 it contained 140 cabins (500 population). It was removed to Butternut Creek, where the fort was burned in 1696. In 1720 it was again moved to Onondaga Creek, and their present reservation in New York State is only a few miles away.

Until this century the Onondaga of the Grand River or Six Nations Reserve, Ontario, Canada, had nine clans: Wolf, Turtle, Bear, Deer, Eel, Beaver, Ball, Plover (Snipe), and Pigeonhawk. The Wolf, Bear, Plover, Ball, and Pigeonhawk clans each have only one federal chieftainship; the Beaver, Turtle, and Eel clans have two federal chieftainships, while the Deer clan has three. The marked difference in the quota of chieftainships may be due to the adoption of other clans and chieftainships which have long been extinct. In the Iroquois ceremonial and social assemblies that exist to the present time, the Onondaga tribe itself constitutes a tribal phratry, or subdivision, while the Mohawk and the Seneca together form a second, and the Oneida and Cayuga (originally) and later the Tuscarora formed the third tribal phratry. The functions of the Onondaga phratry are in many respects similar to those of a judge holding court with a jury.

In the middle of the seventeenth century the Onondaga population was 1,700, but during the eighteenth century the tribe divided. Part of the tribe stayed loyal to the League of Five Nations' historic friendship with the British, while others, under the direct influence of the French Catholic missions on the St. Lawrence River, Canada, migrated there to form small Iroquois colonies. By 1751 about 800 Onondaga were said to be living in Canada. On the outbreak of the American Revolution nearly all the New York Onondaga, together with the majority of the other Iroquois tribes, joined the British; and at the close of the war the British granted them a tract of land on the Grand River, Ontario, Canada, where a portion of them still live mixed with other Iroquois groups. The rest are still in New York State, with the greatest number living on the Onondaga Reservation and the others with the Seneca and Tuscarora on several reservations.

In 1906, those in New York were reported as numbering 553; in 1920, 510 were reported from the Onondaga Reservation alone. On the Six Nations Reserve, in Ontario, about 400 out of a total Iroquois population of 5,400 were reported as Onondaga in 1955. In 1956, 894 Iroquois were reported from the Onondaga Reservation, the greater proportion of these of Onondaga descent, although most tribal members have some white ancestors and some ancestors from other Iroquoian tribes. In 1973, 560 Onondaga were reported among the Six Nations at Grand River, Ontario. In 2000, the single-tribe respondents were 2,130. The Onondaga in New York and Ontario continue to practice the Longhouse ceremonials, including the Midwinter and Harvest rites. The New York Onondaga Reservation remains at the center of traditional Iroquois political and legislative life.

Below: **Onondaga longhouse, Six Nations Indian Reserve near Brantford, Ontario, Canada, seen in August 1990. This longhouse is one of four on the reserve, where some Iroquois people participate in their religion and ritual dramas. Note the kitchen and cookhouse to the right; part of the latter's construction is over 150 years old.**

PAPOOSE

Above: **Ojibwa (Chippewa) or Potawatomi baby, Wisconsin, c. 1905, showing the protective wooden hoop characteristic of Woodland cradle boards; and the decorative cloth securing bands, unlike the laced bag used on cradles by the Northern Ojibwa and Cree of Canada.**

Below: **This couple is probably Prairie Band Potawatomi or Kickapoo, who were in part resettled in northeastern Kansas. The woman wears a cloth skirt with fine ribbon appliqué and silver brooches. The man wears moccasins beaded in the style popular with the resettled Woodland tribes in Kansas and Oklahoma.**

An Algonkian-speaking tribe that probably split from the Ojibwa and Ottawa. The ancient home of the Potawatomi was evidently the Lower Peninsula of Michigan, but in about 1680 they were driven to the Door Peninsula near Green Bay, Wisconsin, on the west side of Lake Michigan. During the eighteenth century they spread south to the present Milwaukee, Wisconsin, area and the St. Joseph River. By 1790 they had scattered at various times from the Mississippi across the northern tributaries of the Illinois River and through southern Michigan to the Detroit area. Their villages were usually established on the edge of the forest adjacent to prairies and lakes. They grew squash, beans, and corn (maize), collected plant foods, and hunted deer, elk, and buffalo. The Potawatomi shared the common Algonkian dual division of clan and social organization, and their beliefs about the spirit world included the curative Midewiwin, the Grand Medicine Lodge Society similar to those of the Ojibwa and Menomini.

Historically, the Potawatomi first aligned themselves with the French against the English and during the American Revolution with the English against the Americans, until a general peace in about 1815, after which they changed rapidly. Forced out of their homelands, they mainly withdrew west across the Mississippi River. In 1841 most of the "Potawatomi of the Woods" from southern Michigan and northern Indiana, already partly acculturated (assimilated to white ways), moved to Kansas, although a few bands, such as the Potawatomi of Huron and Pokagon, remained behind. The Illinois-Wisconsin Potawatomi moved to a reservation in Iowa and from there to one in Kansas, thus combining the Woods and Prairie bands. The most acculturated tribal members moved to a new reservation in Indian Territory, now Oklahoma, in 1867. A number of other groups, probably multitribal and multiethnic and small in number, have survived in various locations to the present time.

Their early population was about 9,000 before a decline due to diseases, warfare, and absorption into other groups. Their present distribution, by no means all Potawatomi and many no longer living within these communities, is as follows: "Prairie band" near Mayetta, Kansas, about 2,000, plus a number with the Kickapoo near Horton; the "Citizen Potawatomi" of Cleveland and Pottawatomie Counties, Oklahoma, locally 3,000; the Hannahville Community in Upper Michigan, 300; two settlements in Forest County, Wisconsin, 400; two groups in southern Michigan, Potawatomi of Huron and Pokagon, 400; and a few found with the Menomini and Winnebago, 100.

In Canada there are substantial numbers with Ojibwa and Ottawa at Walpole Island, Sarnia, Kettle Point, and other locations in Ontario. Their total population given in 1970 was 4,626 in the United States and 863 in Canada. In 1970, fewer than 1,000 people still spoke the Potawatomi language. (For 2000 census figures, see the chart at right.)

The most traditional groups, the Forest County Wisconsin and Prairie band Kansas divisions of the tribe, benefit from successful gaming and entertainment enterprises. The Wisconsin group retained the Medicine Dance society, War Dance, and the Dream or Drum Dance, a variant of the Plains Grass Dance that spread through the woodlands promoting friendship. The ceremony revolves around a large decorated drum that is treated with great reverence and symbolizes friendship, even with whites. Both the Wisconsin and Kansas groups have the Peyote cult, which spread north during the early reservation period. The Peyote cult is a part-Christian and part-Indian religion that involves consuming peyote buttons, a mild hallucinogen, during night-long rituals sometimes held in a tipi to aid the sick. Some Kansas Potawatomi are members of the Kenekuk Church, founded by a Kickapoo holy man in the nineteenth century. They have sponsored large pan-Indian powwows in recent times on their reservation near Mayetta and participate in similar events each year on the nearby Kickapoo Reservation (the two tribes are now much intermarried). In past years, the Potawatomi excelled in ribbonwork and beadwork. Their dress costumes are stylistically similar to the Sauk, Fox, Kickapoo, and other central Algonkians.

Mesquakie (Fox) youth, c. 1890. In this studio photograph, the boy wears a roach hair ornament, beaded apron, belt, cloth leggings, knee garters, and front flap moccasins.

SAUK

An Algonkian people very closely related to the Fox or Mesquakie, formerly living in the vicinity of Green Bay, Wisconsin, toward the end of the seventeenth century. Their traditional subsistance was identical with that of the Fox, combining hunting with growing corn (maize), beans, and squash. Their social organization consisted of about twelve clans organized patrilineally (through the father's line), whose functions were to arrange the sacred medicine pack ceremonies. Disputes with French traders led to a confederation of the Sauks and the Foxes and their migration south from Wisconsin to present-day Iowa and parts of northern Illinois.

Their treaties with the U.S. government in the early nineteenth century, which ceded their lands in Illinois and Wisconsin, were not agreed to by all Sauk and Fox bands; this led to the Black Hawk War of 1832, when they attempted to reestablish control of an old village site near Rock Island, Illinois. Hopelessly outnumbered, Black Hawk and his warriors were finally driven back into Iowa. In 1837, the combined tribes ceded their Iowa lands and were assigned to a reservation in Kansas; but factional disputes resulted in a band of Fox settling at Tama, Iowa, where they remain separate. The remaining Sauk with a few Fox removed from Kansas to Oklahoma (then Indian

Territory) and were assigned lands between the Cimarron River and the north fork of the Canadian River, except for one small group who retained land near the Kansas-Nebraska border. The Sauks' interaction with the U.S. government in the first half of the nineteenth century led to a division between the so-called British band and a faction friendly to the United States led by Keokuk and his followers.

The present descendants of the Oklahoma Sac and Fox live around allotted lands near Stroud and Cushing, Oklahoma, were reported as 996 in 1950, when the small group near White Cloud, Kansas, numbered 129 (see page 46 for 2000 census numbers). The Oklahoma bands have an annual powwow of the pan-Indian type near the tribal administration complex south of Stroud, Oklahoma, each summer, which incorporates what little remains of traditional Indian culture and reinforces their tribal unity. The Oklahoma Sauk are officially called the "Sac and Fox tribe of the Missouri."

Above: **A Sauk and Fox woman shows her ribbonwork at the Mashantucket Pequot Powwow, Connecticut, September 1995.**

MESQUAKIE (FOX)

Early reports located the Mesquakie along the Fox River in Wisconsin, living in rectangular bark lodges large enough to accommodate several families, with

Right: Sauk or Mesquakie (Fox) warrior of c. 1867 wearing a head roach, widely used by eastern and midwestern tribes and usually constructed of porcupine and deer hair, with a braided woolen turban, silver earrings, and bear claw necklace.

Far right: Mesquakie (Fox) children, c. 1890. The boy holds a pipe.

Below: Sauk and Mesquakie (Fox) warrior of the mid-eighteenth century with head shaved except for a small braid to secure the roach (of porcupine and deer hair, or turkey beards). In early times this was much smaller than the still widely used dancer's roach. The spines of the roach feathers are covered with quill-wrapped sticks or rawhide. His sashes of natural fiber are interspaced with trade beads, a trade silver gorget and nose and ear rings. Shaven-headed warriors were known as far west as the Pawnee and Eastern Sioux.

shelves several feet off the ground on both sides for sleeping and food storage. They maintained extensive gardens where squash, beans, and corn were grown, usually tended by women. After the harvest was completed, the grain and dried squash were cached (stored in a hiding place) and the men went on their winter hunts, sometimes making excursions into buffalo country. They also hunted deer and other game. In recent times the Mesquakie generally lived in wigwams (pole-frame houses usually covered with bark) or wickiups (from the Fox word for "house," in this case a tipi made of mat-covered bent poles). Their name for themselves is "Red Earth People," which distinguished them from their kinsmen the Sauk, the "Yellow Earth People."

The Mesquakie seem to have encountered French missionaries after about 1640 but were later hostile to the French, who in 1746 drove them west from their original homes on the Fox to the Wisconsin River, where they remained until withdrawing across the Mississippi to Iowa at the beginning of the nineteenth century. They united with the Sauk after the Black Hawk War of 1832 in Iowa and in 1842 removed to Kansas. A number, mostly Mesquakie, instead established themselves near Tama, Iowa, and have remained there to the present time, their settlement for years a stronghold of traditional Indian beliefs and religious practices. The present population of the Iowa Fox is about 1,300, although a number live in industrial communities away from the reservation. They have been noted in the past for the production of fine

beadwork, ribbonwork, and metalwork and are still producers of fine ceremonial and dance costume. A number of Mesquakie also accompanied their kinsmen the Sauk to Kansas and Oklahoma and are officially the "Sac and Fox" tribe because of their combined dealings with the U.S. government during the nineteenth century. Their language is still spoken by a number of the tribe at Tama, Iowa. Confusingly, the Tama Mesquakie are officially called the "Sac and Fox of the Mississippi in Iowa."

Above: **Sauk elm bark house, c. 1880. Shorter than but of similar construction to Iroquois longhouses, Sauk and Fox bark lodges formed villages of up to around ninety houses in the mid-eighteenth century. A few were still being built in the 1880s after removal to Indian Territory (present-day Oklahoma).**

Right: **Two Iowa Mesquakie youths, c. 1900, wearing beaded sashes, knee bands, and breechcloths. The young man on the left wears a head roach of either porcupine hair or turkey beards.**

Far right: **Sauk and Fox (Mesquakie) women wearing shirts with ribbonwork decoration. Rock Island Powwow, 1959.**

CENSUS 2000

The numbers recorded for the Sauk and Mesquakie were:

Sac and Fox Tribe of the Mississippi in Iowa	1,281
Sac and Fox Nation of Missouri in Kansas and Nebraska	79
Sac and Fox Nation, Oklahoma	533
Sac and Fox	2,313
Total	4,206

KICKAPOO

An Algonkian-speaking tribe closely related to the Sauk and Fox. The movements of the Kickapoo were so frequent that they cannot be associated with any one specific area, but it is probable that when first known to whites in 1660–1700, their home was in southern Wisconsin. Hostile to the French, they were later friendly with the English during the Revolution and the War of 1812; and a few joined Black Hawk in 1832. Both bands were in Missouri by the early nineteenth century and moved then to northeastern Kansas (1832–34); but some, wishing to remain free from white restrictions, were already moving to Texas. These ultimately decamped to Mexico, where a settlement was established near Nacimiento, Coahuila. There, a basic forest Algonkian culture was reestablished with modifications dictated by their new environment. In 1873, one hundred or more Kickapoo from Kansas moved to Indian Territory to a reservation based along the North Canadian River in present Lincoln and Pottawatomi Counties, Oklahoma, while about 250 remained on their Kansas reservation near Horton. These three communities continue today. The Oklahoma Kickapoo number about 500, the Kansas group, 400 (combined total given as 1,249 in 1970), and the Mexican band, 400. In 1990, the Kickapoo totaled about 3,000. In 2000, the census reported 5,116 Kickapoo and part Kickapoo.

SHAWNEE

ALGONKIAN

One of the most important language families of North America, spoken aboriginally from the Canadian Maritimes to North Carolina and inland to the Great Plains. This language family seems to be divided into three components: the divergent Plains branch, made up of the Blackfeet, Cheyenne, and Arapaho; a Central branch comprising the Cree-Montagnais-Naskapi group, the Ojibwa-Ottawa-Potawatomi group, and the Fox-Menomini-Shawnee-Illinois-Miami group; and finally an Eastern branch. The Eastern branch is not fully classified, since several tribes became extinct before linguistic records could be made, but the following divisions may be reasonably accurate: Micmac, Malecite-Passamaquoddy, Abenaki (two dialects), Nipmuck-Pocumtuck, Massachuset, Narraganset, Mohegan-Pequot, Montauk, Unquachog (Long Island), Quiripi (Connecticut), Mohican, Delaware (two dialects), Nanticoke, Powhatan, and Carolina. Of all these Eastern dialects only Micmac is extensively spoken today. The name of the whole group derives from the Algonkin (Algonquin) proper, a branch of the Northern Ojibwa in Quebec. Census 2000 recorded 1,107 "Algonquians."

An Algonkian people who were frequently divided and moved many times. The original home of the Shawnee was probably the Cumberland River in Tennessee. During the eighteenth century, the Muskingum and Scioto River valleys in the Ohio country were their primary home. At that time the Shawnee were a major frontier tribe actively engaged in warfare against the encroaching white settlers. However, they had also settled in various parts of Pennsylvania during the early part of that century, attracted by the English trade. One band, the Saluda, even settled for a time among the Creek of the Southeast, driving the Yuchi from the middle Savannah (Georgia) region but subsequently rejoined a main body of the tribe in Pennsylvania. The Shawnee tribe had five component parts, perhaps originally separate tribes—Chillicothe (Calaka), Kispokotha (Kispoko), Piqua or Pickaway (Pekowi), Sawekela or Hathawekela (Thawikila), and Makostrake (Mekoce)—but their functions seem to have been largely political and ritual. They combined hunting with agriculture for their subsistence but were strongly oriented toward the fur trade from the early eighteenth century. Their supreme being Creator was female.

The Shawnee were consistently opposed to white settlement west of the Appalachian Mountains, switching their alliances between France and Britain as a result. They joined the Pontiac uprising against the British (1763), fought against the Virginians in Lord Dunmore's War (1774), and later fought the Americans in the Revolution. They took up arms against the Americans again under the leadership of Tecumseh and Tenskwatawa (The Prophet) at Tippecanoe and in the War of 1812. However, by this time constant warfare had exhausted and split them. Contact with whites over a long period had resulted in a mixed culture similar to those of other Midwest tribes. By the late eighteenth century, a large body of Shawnee and others had begun to settle in Spanish territory, present-day Missouri, but the main body of the tribe was still in Indiana and Ohio on the White, Auglaize, and Miami rivers.

By the 1830s, most of the Indiana Shawnee bands, with some Missouri bands (later known as Black Bob's band), had reunited on a reservation on the Kansas River in northeastern Kansas. Others, wishing to be free of white influence, left for Arkansas, Texas, and beyond, later being known as "Absentee" Shawnee, as they were separate from the main body of the tribe still living in Kansas. In 1832, a mixed band of Seneca-Iroquois and Shawnee coming direct from Ohio moved to northeastern Indian Territory, now Ottawa County, Oklahoma. In 1870, following the Civil War, the main body of the tribe moved from Kansas to the Cherokee Nation, Indian Territory, while the Absentee Shawnee and Black Bob's band obtained lands between the North Canadian and Canadian Rivers in Indian Territory, along with the Potawatomi.

The Ottawa County Shawnee separated from the Seneca in 1867; their descendants, known as the Eastern Shawnee, number about 600. The Cherokee-Shawnee or Loyal-Shawnee of Craig County, Oklahoma, number about 1,100; and the Absentee Shawnee number about 1,000 in Pottawatomie and Cleveland Counties. One community at Little Axe were a relatively conservative group until recently, maintaining traditional Shawnee rituals such as the War Dance and the Bread Dance. The Loyal and Eastern bands are largely of mixed descent and have been highly acculturated (assimilated to white ways) for generations. The 1970 U.S. census counted 2,208 Shawnee—probably an underestimation when considering the Census 2000 figure of 5,773.

Most present-day Shawnees belong to federally recognized tribes (such as the Absentee Shawnee and the Eastern Shawnee Tribe), have state recognition (The Loyal Shawnee), or are petitioning for federal recognition (Shawnee Nation United Remnant Band, recognized by the state of Ohio, and the Piqua Sect of Ohio). Federal tribal status affords certain rights and priveleges previously gained through treaties.

Absentee Shawnee Tribe of Indians of Oklahoma	1,701
Eastern Shawnee	1,022
Shawnee	2,987
Piqua Sept of Ohio Shawnee	63
Total	5,773

WESTERN ABENAKI

The designation "Western Abenaki" is now given to the Algonkians who spoke one dialect and inhabited the upper Connecticut River valley in New Hampshire, Massachusetts, and Vermont. They were sometimes called Sokoki, including perhaps the Pennacook on the Merrimack River and the Missisquoi on Lake Champlain. Like their Eastern Abenaki relatives, they gradually abandoned New England for French Canada after King Philip's War, 1675–76 and finally settled at the St. Francis Mission and Bécancour in Quebec. Recently, a mixed-ancestry group living around Swanton, Vermont, have also claimed Abenaki ancestry. During the nineteenth century many Abenakis made split-ash baskets to be sold to whites; some basket examples remain in museums. The Abenaki Nation of Missiquoi numbered 2,385 in Census 2000.

ABENAKI

Algonkians of central Maine. The Abenaki are divided into several subdivisions, of which the Pigwacket (Pequawket), Norridgewock, and Penobscot are the largest—the latter often given separate status. The explorer Champlain passed through their territory in 1604, and thenceforth they were under French influence and hostile to the English. They suffered as a result, the Norridgewock and Pequawket divisions being almost wiped out. Much reduced, they withdrew in the late seventeenth century to French Canada, where they settled ultimately at Bécancour and St. Francis. From there they retaliated against New England settlements, often adopting white captives. The Abenaki took on Catholicism after their settlement in French Canada led to an abandonment of Native religion. The Maine Abenakis have merged with the Western Abenaki at St. Francis, but the Penobscot remained in Maine after making peace with the English in 1759. Their descendants remain in Old Town, along with some Passamaquoddy.

BROTHERTON or BROTHERTOWN

Two separate groups of remnant New England Algonkians. The first were Mohican, Wappinger, Pequot, Mohegan, Narraganset, and Montauk who moved to lands given them by the Oneida in Madison and Oneida Counties, New York, under a Native minister, Samson Occom (1723–92). The second group were Raritan-Delawares from a reservation in New Jersey called Brotherton in Burlington County, who joined the first group in New York in 1802. The combined group moved to Wisconsin in 1833 under the name Brotherton, and their descendants (Census 2000 records 622) live near Fond du Lac.

CONOY or PISCATAWAY

An Algonkian tribe related to the Nanticoke who lived on the western shore of Chesapeake Bay and along the Potomac River. They were in conflict with Maryland colonists after 1634 and harassed by the Susquehannocks from the north. They were forced to leave with some remaining Nanticokes under Iroquois protection, first to

Pennsylvania, then to Chenango and Owego, New York. Some seem to have remained in Maryland, presumably intermixing with whites and African Americans. Census 2000 records 2,538 part and pure Piscataway.

ILLINI or ILLINOIS

A group of Algonkian-speaking tribes more or less closely connected, who lived principally along the Mississippi and Illinois Rivers, including the Michigamea, Cahokia, Kaskaskia, Moingwena, Peoria, and Tamaroa. Their language was closest to that of the Miami. As the population of these groups dwindled they often re-formed in new locations. They were an agricultural people dependent upon corn; they also gathered wild foods and hunted game, including buffalo.

Their first contacts with Europeans were with the expedition of Marquette and Jolliet in about 1675; they soon came under French influence, and their decline followed quickly due to smallpox and Iroquois attacks. A group called Peoria in Oklahoma are their descendants.

LOWER CONNECTICUT RIVER TRIBES

A number of small tribes in present-day Connecticut, in contact with English settlers from 1639 onward, including the Tunxis near Hartford, Podunk near Windsor, Wangunk near Wethersfield, and Quinnipiac near New Haven. Several historians incorrectly added them to the so-called Wappinger group, but they may have shared a separate Algonkian dialect (now called Quiripi) with the lower Housatonic River groups. They may have numbered around 2,200 in the early seventeenth century, but they diminished rapidly and sold their lands to English settlers until only a few remained.

MASSACHUSETT

A group of villages around Boston, Massachusetts, between Salem and Brockton along the coast, and as far inland as the Concord River. They probably spoke the same Algonkian dialect as the Pawtucket. Visited by several European voyagers before contact with the English settlement at Plymouth in 1621, the Massachusetts may have numbered 3,000 at the time of contact but were reduced rapidly by smallpox and other epidemics. Puritans soon gathered their remaining numbers into small villages

Above: **Penobscot Clown Dancer, nineteenth century. The only Eastern Abenaki group to remain in Maine was one of the few pockets of Eastern seaboard peoples who retained elements of traditional culture late enough to be recorded by ethnographers. The Clown or Trading Dance was a popular gaming ceremony performed at night; the clown wears a deer mask, mooseskin coat, and buckskin moccasins with large U-shaped instep vamps. Census 2000 recorded 3,801 pure and part Penobscot.**

Above: **Mohegan, c. 1880. Northeastern Algonkians including the Mohegans and Narragansetts all but lost Native dress by the 19th century. Male dress for special occasions sometimes included a beaded cloth cape as a symbol of rank. The upright feathered headdress with beaded band may be descended from an earlier form or copied from the popular Western war bonnet.**

of Christianized "Praying Indians," and these intermarried with African Americans during the eighteenth century. A few people of mixed descent survived down to the twentieth century near Canton and Mansfield in Norfolk County, Massachusetts.

MIAMI

An Algonkian people related to the Illini centered in present-day Indiana along the Wabash and Eel River drainages during the eighteenth century, when they were reduced to three small tribes: the Wea, Piankashaw, and Miami proper. They probably came originally from the Fox River area of Wisconsin. Like other tribes of the area they lived in oval lodges covered with cattail mats, bark, or hides, in small villages along river banks, with a mixed farming and hunting economy. The Miami supported the British in the Revolution and continued resistance against American forces until defeated by Anthony Wayne at Fallen Timbers in 1794. After the Treaty of Greenville (1795) they remained at peace but declined rapidly in numbers. Between 1832 and 1840 they moved to reservations in Kansas, where the Wea and Piankashaw united with remaining Illini under the name Peoria. The Peoria and Miami removed in 1867 to Indian Territory, now Oklahoma, where two mixed-descent groups remain in Ottawa County. A few remained in Indiana near Peru, where some 500 mixed-descent people are said to survive.

MOHEGAN

An Algonkian people who occupied the Thames River valley and its branches in Connecticut, often confused with the Mohican. They were closely related to and perhaps once the same people as the Pequot. The Mohegan separated from the Pequot after the destruction of that tribe by white colonists aided by coastal Indians and Mohegans led by Uncas in 1637. They have continued to live in Connecticut, although some joined the Brotherton and the Scaticook. Some 100 descendants still live near Uncasville, Connecticut. Census 2000 identifies 2,428 Mohegan descendants, of which 1,248 are part Mohegan. Mohegans grew corn, hunted, and traded with Long Island Indians for wampum shell money, used also by white settlers, which drew them into the European money exchange at an early date.

MONTAUK

A group of tribes occasionally termed "Metoac" and consisting of Algonkians of Long Island, New York, excepting those at the extreme western end, who are classed with the Delaware. They were famous in history for the production of wampum shell money, which they traded to mainland tribes until the production was taken over by white settlers. They survived King Philip's War (1675–76) relatively undisturbed, but they were attacked by the Narragansets and decreased in numbers due to diseases; after 1775 some joined the Brotherton in New York. Remaining on Long Island were the Shinnecock (2,758, including part Shinnecock), who still retain a reservation near Southampton; the Poosepatuck, whose descendants own land at the mouth of the Mastic River (447); the Montauk proper (680), near Montauk Point and East Hampton; the Matinecock on the north shore in Nassau County (84); and the Setauket, a few (447) descendants of whom were once found in Suffolk County but are now no longer reported.

NANTICOKE

An Algonkian people of Delaware and Maryland on both sides of Chesapeake Bay and the north bank of the Potomac River. The Nanticoke comprise several subgroups, including the Nanticoke (proper), Wicocomoco, Choptank, Pocomoke, the Wicomiss or Ozinies, and the Patuxent. European contact increased after the establishment of Jamestown in 1607; thereafter disputes with the Maryland colonists led to continual outbreaks of violence. Many Nanticoke were forced to leave under Iroquois protection for the Chenango River at Otsiningo—present-day Binghamton, New York—along with the Conoy and others. The last of these immigrant Nanticoke were counted among the Iroquois at Six Nations, Ontario, or Buffalo Creek, New York, and lost their separate identity. Those who remained in parts of their old country intermarried with African Americans at an early date. Nanticoke descendants—of whom, in Census 2000, 1,601 plus 749 "Nanticoke Lenni-Linape" are recorded —hold a Pan-Indian Powwow each year near Millsboro, Delaware.

NARRAGANSETT

Algonkian people of Rhode Island, west of Narragansett Bay. They seem to have been closely related to the Niantic,

MENOMINI (MENOMINEE)

An Algonkian tribe located on or near the Menominee River, Wisconsin. They probably first encountered the French around 1634 and were usually firm friends of the French, with whom they often intermarried. In 1854 they were restricted to a reservation in present Menominee County, Wisconsin, where their descendants remain. In 1961, the reservation was terminated, but it was restored in 1973. In 1992 they had 7,000 members, half on their reservation. In 2000 the figure was 9,840, including part Menominee.

Below: **Louise Amor of the Menomini, c. 1915. She is wearing a skirt and blanket decorated with fine bands of cut and fold ribbonwork characteristic of the southern Woodland tribes.**

with whom they ultimately merged. They had a population of several thousand, which escaped the first smallpox epidemic of 1617, but many died in 1633. They became friends of the English in 1636 after Roger Williams laid the foundations of the Rhode Island colony. They remained on good terms with whites until King Philip's War (1675–76), when they joined the opposition and lost 1,000 people at the Great Swamp Fight near Kingston. Some fled the country, and others joined the Niantic. Since then they have lived in the same area, although many left and joined the Brotherton or Mohegan during the eighteenth century. Their descendants are still found in Rhode Island.

NIPMUC or NIPMUCK

Native villagers in central Massachusetts who spoke an Algonkian dialect connected with that of the Pocumtuck, west of the Connecticut River. The Nipmuc were greatly weakened by European diseases, and their survivors settled in white villages. Some probably took part in King Philip's War, 1675–76, after which only a few survived. Some descendants remain on the Hassanimisco Reservation near Grafton, and a few people near Dudley and Webster may also have Nipmuc ancestry.

NORTH CAROLINA ALGONKIANS

Tribes famous for their connection with the Raleigh colonists, who established a settlement in 1585–87 on Roanoke Island at the mouth of Albemarle Sound in North Carolina. The artist John White made watercolor picturesof their villages, dwellings, fishing techniques, and some individual studies. The main tribal groups included the Weapemeoc, Moratok, Secotan, Pamlico, Bear River, Pomeiooc, Machapunga, Croatoan (Hatteras), and Chowanoc. During the eighteenth and nineteenth centuries they seem to have merged with African-American populations, and only a few of mixed descent survived. The Lumbee of Robeson County, North Carolina, claim the ancestry of the coastal tribes and Raleigh colonists, but this is unsupported by historical evidence.

PASSAMAQUODDY

Related to the Malecite, this people remained in Maine after the British conquest of Canada in 1759. They were located on Passamaquoddy Bay and along the St. Croix River. Their culture and history are similar to those of other Maritime Algonkian groups. About 1,000 descendants live on three state reservations near Princeton and Eastport. A few have retained their language and a little craftwork, but Native religious traditions have largely fallen into disuse. Formerly they were hunters of moose and caribou, but they also ate clams, lobsters, porpoise, and salmon. In recent times they have grown potatoes and other crops. Along with their close relatives, they once formed a loose, Iroquois-type confederacy called Wabanaki.

PAUGUSSETT or LOWER HOUSATONIC RIVER TRIBES

A group of four small tribes living on the Housatonic River, Connecticut, during the early seventeenth century: the Paugusset, Pequannock, Potatuck, and Weantinock or Wawyachtonok. They diminished in numbers due to white epidemics and were pressured into land sales. A small mission village, Schaghticoke or Scaticook, was established by Mahwee, a Pequot, early in the eighteenth century. It became a refuge for a mixed tribal group, mostly Paugusset. Perhaps fifty or so descendants still identify as Scaticook, with four families resident on their small reservation near Bulls Bridge, Kent, Connecticut, in 1988. A few other Paugusset descendants live on the Golden Hill reservation, Connecticut.

PENNACOOK or PAWTUCKET

An Algonkian people of the Merrimack River, New Hampshire, and parts of adjacent Maine and Massachusetts, perhaps exceeding 2,000 people. Their history is similar to that of both the Western Abenakis, with whom they are usually classified, and the Eastern Abenakis of Maine. They were defeated in 1676 at the close of King Philip's War, and their survivors withdrew to Canada, uniting with the Abenakis at St. Francis, Quebec.

PEQUOT

An Algonkian tribe, perhaps once one with the Mohegans, together numbering more than 4,000. They occupied eastern Connecticut, particularly around the Mystic River.

CENSUS 2000	
Croatoan	77
Narragansett	2,137
Nipmuc	
Hassanamisco Band of the Nipmuc Nation	11
Chaubunagungameg Nipmuc	1
Nipmuc	654
Total	666
Schaghticoke	256
Passamaquoddy	
Passamaquoddy	2,397
Pleasant Point Passamaquoddy	1
Total	2,398

Opposite: **Winnebago Young Eagle Chakshebneeneik wearing a bandolier bag and beaded shirt, c. 1890.**

Below: **A photo of Winnebago Standing Buffalo, c. 1860s. He wears a head roach set back on his head, and metal earrings, and holds an eagle feather fan. He also wears hide leggings, moccasins, aprons, and armbands, wristlets, and knee garters with fur drops, which probably confirms his status as a warrior.**

Their subsistence came from hunting, collecting, corn harvesting, waterfowl, and shellfish. They lived in villages of several houses of bark-covered saplings, sometimes large enough for a number of families. The Pequot seem to have been at war with their neighbors at the time of first European settlement, which they strongly resisted. They were defeated by a combined body of English, Mohegan, and Narraganset in 1637, with their principal settlement completely destroyed. Many were sold into slavery in the West Indies, and others fled west. A few obtained two land grants from the English in New London—Mushantuxet in 1667 and Lantern Hill in 1683, near Ledyard, Connecticut—that still exist as reservations. About 100 people live there and constitute one of the few surviving Indian groups of southern New England. A gaming operation has recently brought immense wealth to the Mushantuxet band (Mashantucket Pequot).

POCOMTUC or POCUMTUCK
Algonkian villagers of west central Massachusetts from Agawam in the south to Deerfield in the north. They may have been connected to the Nipmuc or Wappinger. Their main settlement was Fort Hill, Franklin County, destroyed by the Mohawk in 1666. They joined the hostilities in King Philip's War; at its close their survivors fled west to the Hudson and ultimately to the Abenaki at St. Francis, Quebec, where they disappeared as a separate group.

POWHATAN
A large and important collection of Algonkian groups in the Tidewater portion of Virginia. From 1607 they were in contact and ultimately in conflict with the English colonists at Jamestown. Powhatan was their paramount chief, from whom the whole group have been named the Powhatan confederacy. They cultivated corn, which was stored on raised platforms after harvesting; they also hunted, fished, and gathered wild plant foods. They wore buckskin garments, frequently fringed, painted, and decorated with shells. Wars with the colonists in 1622 and 1644 broke Powhatan power, after which they were restricted to English land grants, exposed to harassment by Iroquois and Susquehannocks (Conestogas), and retaliated against by whites for crimes allegedly often

committed by these northern Indians. By the end of the seventeenth century they mainly worked as hunters, scouts, and servants, with considerable intermarriage with whites following the famous Pocahontas–John Rolfe marriage and later with African-American slaves. While many Powhatan people have survived, only the Pamunkey and Mattaponi subtribes can claim unbroken links with their seventeenth-century ancestors.

WAMPANOAG or POKANOKET

Algonkian people of southern Massachusetts and Rhode Island, including those on the coast below Marshfield and on Cape Cod, Martha's Vineyard, Nantucket, and part of Narragansett Bay. The Nauset of Cape Cod and Sakonnet of Rhode Island are sometimes considered separately. The Wampanoag were known to Europeans at least as early as 1602 and helped the Mayflower Pilgrims establish their settlements after 1620. Wampanoag remnants settled in various locations, mostly in Bristol and Barnstable Counties, Massachusetts. Groups in Mashpee and Gay Head (Martha's Vineyard) survive today.

WAPPINGER and LOWER HUDSON RIVER TRIBES

They lived on the east bank of the Hudson River near Poughkeepsie, New York, but "Wappinger" may also describe related groups as far south as Manhattan Island. Some joined the Stockbridge in Massachusetts and the Nanticoke and Delaware in New York and ultimately disappeared as a separate group.

WINNEBAGO or HO-CHUNK

A Siouan enclave largely surrounded by Algonkians, the Winnebago lived between the Rock and Black rivers in southern Wisconsin. They were noted by the French as early as 1634 and usually aided the French during the colonial wars. Many had removed to southern Minnesota by 1855 and in 1874 moved again, to a reservation in Nebraska purchased from the Omaha, where many of their descendants remain. However, not all the Winnebagos left Wisconsin, and others returned from Nebraska to form several small communities around Tomah and Black River Falls, Wisconsin. These two divisions remain today and have recently achieved great success in the gaming and hotel industries, with which they provide revenue for both themselves and Wisconsin.

GLOSSARY

Allotment. Legal process, c. 1880s–1930s, by which land on reservations not allocated to Indian families was made available to whites.

Anthropomorphic. Having the shape of, or having the characteristics of, humans; usually refers to an animal or god.

Appliqué. Decorative technique involving sewing down quills (usually porcupine) and seed beads onto hide or cloth using two threads, resulting in a flat mosaic surface.

Apron. Male apparel, front and back, which replaced the breechcloth for festive costume during the nineteenth and twentieth centuries.

Bandolier bag. A prestige bag with a shoulder strap, usually with heavy beadwork, worn by men and sometimes women at tribal dances. Common among the Ojibwe and other Woodland groups.

Birch bark. An important resource, especially in the East, North, and Northwest. Strong, thick bark was used for canoes and various wigwam coverings. It was used as well for a wide variety of containers that were also adapted for the European souvenir trade by the addition of colored porcupine quills, such as those produced by the Mi'kmaq, and later by the Ojibwe and Odawa of the Great Lakes area.

Buckskin. Hide leather from animals of the deer family—deer (white-tailed deer in the East, mule deer in the West), moose, or elk (wapiti)—used for clothing. Less commonly used for dress were the hides of buffalo, bighorn sheep, Dall sheep, mountain goat, and caribou.

Coiling. A method of making pottery in the American Southwest, in which walls of a vessel are built up by adding successive ropelike coils of clay.

Confederacy. A group of peoples or villages bound together politically or for defense (e.g., Iroquois, Creek).

Cradles. There were three main types of cradle employed across the continent: the cradle board of the Woodland tribes (cloth or skin attached to a wooden board with a protecting angled bow), the baby-carrier of the Plains (a bag on a frame or triangular hood with a cloth base folded around the baby), and a flat elliptical board covered with skin or cloth, with a shallow bag or hide straps, of the Plateau.

Drum or Dream Dance. A variation of the Plains Grass Dance adopted by the Santee Sioux, Chippewa, and Menomini during the nineteenth century. Among these groups the movement had religious features that advocated friendship, even with whites.

Hairpipes. Tubular bone beads made by whites and traded to the Indians, often made up into vertical and horizontal rows called breastplates.

Housepost. Part of the structure of a Northwest Coast house to support the roof, often carved with family or ancestral emblems.

Kachinas. Supernatural beings impersonated by costumed Pueblo peoples in religious ceremonial. Dressed kachina dolls instruct children to recognize the different spirits.

Kiva. The structure, often underground, that serves as a ceremonial chamber for Pueblo peoples in the Southwest. Each village usually has several kivas.

Lazy stitch. A Plains technique of sewing beads to hide or cloth, giving a final ridged or arch effect in lanes about eight or ten beads wide.

Leggings. Male or female, covering ankle and leg to the knee or thigh (male), usually buckskin or cloth.

Longhouse. The religion of conservative Iroquois, whose rituals still take place in special buildings also called longhouses. These buildings represent the old bark longhouse and a microform of Iroquoia itself.

Medicine bundle. A group of objects, sometimes animal, bird, or mineral, etc., contained in a wrapping of buckskin or cloth, that gave access to considerable spiritual power when opened with the appropriate ritual. Mostly found among the eastern and Plains groups.

Moiety. A ceremonial division of a village, tribe, or nation.

Pan-Indian. Describes the modern mixed intertribal dances, costumes, powwows, and socializing leading to the reinforcement of ethnic and nationalist ties.

Parfleche. A rawhide envelope or box made to contain clothes or meat, often decorated with painted geometrical designs.

Peyote. A stimulant and hallucinogenic substance obtained from the peyote buttons of the mescal cactus.

Peyote Religion. The Native American Church, a part-Native and part-Christian religion originating in Mexico but developed among the Southern Plains tribes in Oklahoma, which has spread to many Native communities.

Potlatch. A status-confirming ceremony among Northwest Coast First Nations.

Powwow. Modern celebration, often intertribal and secular, held on most reservations throughout the year.

Prehistoric. In a Eurocentric view of Indian archaeology, this refers to Indian life and its remains dated before A.D. 1492.

Rancherias. Small reservations in California.

Rawhide. Usually hard, dehaired hide or skin used for parfleche cases, moccasin soles, shields, drum-heads, etc.

Reservation. Government-created lands to which Indian peoples were assigned, removed, or restricted during the nineteenth and twentieth centuries. In Canada they are called reserves.

Roach. A headdress of deer and porcupine hair, very popular for male war-dance attire, which originated among the eastern tribes and later spread among the Plains Indians along with the popular Omaha or Grass Dance, the forerunner of the modern War and Straight dances.

Sinew. The tendon fiber from animals, used by Indians and Inuit as thread for sewing purposes.

Smoked tanning. A buckskin tanning process to maintain the leather in a supple condition.

Sweat lodge. A low, temporary, oval-shaped structure covered with skins or blankets, in which one sits in steam produced by splashing water on heated stones as a method of ritual purification.

Syllabics. A form of European-inspired writing consisting of syllabic characters used by the Cherokee in the nineteenth century and in other forms by the Cree and Inuit.

Termination. Withdrawal of U.S. government recognition of the protected status of, and services due to, an Indian reservation.

Tipi bag. Bags, usually buckskin, used for storage inside tipis.

Tobacco or pipe bag. Bags, usually buckskin, beaded, or quilled with fringing, made by most Plains peoples for men to carry ceremonial tobacco and pipes.

Tribe. A word that arouses controversy, many prefering "Nation" or "People." It means a group of bands linked together genetically, politically, geographically, by religion, or by a common origin myth; but a common language is the main reason. Some "tribal" groups are only so described as a convenient tool for ethnographers studying collectively fragmented groups or collections of small groups of peoples who themselves recognized no such association.

War dance. Popular name for the secular male dances that developed in Oklahoma and other places after the spread of the Grass Dances from the eastern Plains–Prairie tribes, among whom it was connected with war societies. Many tribes had complex war and victory celebrations.

MUSEUMS

The United States naturally has the largest number of museums, with vast holdings of Indian material and art objects. The Peabody Museum of Archaeology and Ethnology at Harvard University, in Cambridge, Massachusetts, has over 500,000 ethnographic objects pertaining to North America, including a large number of Northwest Coast pieces. Many collections of Indian artifacts in major U.S. institutions were assembled by ethnologists and archaeologists who were working for, or contracted to, various major museums, such as Frank Speck and Frances Densmore for the Smithsonian Institution, Washington, D.C., or George Dorsey for the Field Museum of Natural History, Chicago.

Since the sixteenth century, the material culture of the Native peoples of North America has been collected and dispersed around the world. These objects, where they survived, often found their way into European museums, some founded in the eighteenth century. Unfortunately, these objects usually have missing or incomplete documentation, and because such material was collected during the European (British, French, Spanish, Russian) and later American exploration, exploitation, and colonization of North America, these collections may or may not accurately represent Native cultures. Collectors in the early days were usually sailors (Captain Cook), soldiers (Sir John Caldwell), Hudson's Bay Company agents, missionaries, traders, or explorers.

During the twentieth century, a number of museums have developed around the collections of private individuals. The most important was that of George Heye, whose museum was founded in 1916 (opened 1922) and located in New York City. It was called the Museum of the American Indian, Heye Foundation. This collection has now been incorporated into the National Museum of the American Indian, a huge building sited on the Mall in Washington, D.C., scheduled to open in September 2004. Other notable privately owned collections subsequently purchased or presented to scholarly institutions are the Haffenreffer Museum Collection at Brown University, Rhode Island; much of Milford G. Chandler's collection, which is now at the Detroit Institute of Arts; Adolph Spohr's collection at the Buffalo Bill Historical Center, Cody, Wyoming; and the impressive Arthur Speyer collection at the National Museums of Canada, Ottawa.

Many U.S. and Canadian museums and institutions have been active in publishing popular and scholarly ethnographic reports, including the Glenbow-Alberta Institute, the Royal Ontario Museum, Toronto, and, pre-eminently, the Smithsonian Institution, Washington, D.C. Most of the major U.S. museums have organized significant exhibitions of Indian art, and their accompanying catalogs and publications, often with Native input, contain important and valuable information.

In the recent past, a number of Indian-owned and -run museums have come into prominence, such as the Seneca-Iroquois National Museum, Salamanca, New York; the Turtle Museum at Niagara Falls; Woodland Cultural Centre, Brantford, Ontario, Canada; and the Pequot Museum, initiated with funding from the Pequots' successful gaming operation in Connecticut. The Pequots have also sponsored a number of Indian art exhibitions. Many smaller tribal museums are now found on a number of reservations across the United States.

There has also been much comment, debate, and honest disagreement between academics (Indian and non-Indian alike), museum personnel, and historians about the role of museums and the validity of ownership of Indian cultural material in what have been, in the past, non-Native institutions. Certain Indian groups have, through the legal process, won back from museums a number of funerary and religious objects, where these have been shown to be of major importance to living tribes or nations. The Native American Graves and Repatriation Act of 1990, now a federal law, has guided institutions to return artifacts to Native petitioners; some, such as the Field Museum of Chicago, while not strictly bound by this law, have voluntarily returned some remains and continue to negotiate loans and exhanges with various Native American groups. A listing of U.S. museums with Native American resources may be found at http://www.hanksville.org/NAresources/indices/NAmuseums.html.

FURTHER READING

Birchfield, D. L.(General Ed.): *The Encyclopedia of North American Indians,* Marshall Cavendish, 1997.

Brody, H.: *Maps and Dreams,* Jill Norman and Hobhouse Ltd, 1981.

Bruchac, Joseph: *Journal of Jesse Smoke: A Cherokee Boy: Trail of Tears, 1838.* Scholastic, Inc., 2001.

Buller, Laura: *Native Americans: An Inside Look at the Tribes and Traditions,* DK Publishing, Inc., 2001.

Coe, R. T.: *Sacred Circles: Two Thousand Years of North American Indian Art;* Arts Council of GB, 1976.

Cooper, Michael J.: *Indian School: Teaching the White Man's Way,* Houghton MIfflin Company, 1999.

Davis, M. B. (Ed.): *Native America in the Twentieth Century;* Garland Publishing, Inc., 1994.

Dennis, Y. W., Hischfelder, A. B., and Hirschfelder, Y: *Children of Native America Today,* Charlesbridge Publishing, Inc., 2003.

Despard, Yvone: *Folk Art Projects - North America,* Evan-Moor Educational Publishers, 1999.

Downs, D.: *Art of the Florida Seminole and Miccosukee Indians,* University Press of Florida, 1995.

Duncan, K. C.: *Northern Athapaskan Art: A Beadwork Tradition,* Un. Washington Press, 1984.

Ewers, J. C.: *Blackfeet Crafts,* "Indian Handicraft" series; Educational Division, U.S. Bureau of Indian Affairs, Haskell Institute, 1944.

Fenton, W. N.: *The False Faces of the Iroquois,* Un. Oklahoma Press, 1987.

Fleming, P. R., and Luskey, J.: *The North American Indians in Early Photographs,* Dorset Press, 1988.

Frazier, P.: *The Mohicans of Stockbridge,* Un. Nebraska Press, Lincoln, 1992.

Gidmark, D.: *Birchbark Canoe, Living Among the Algonquin,* Firefly Books, 1997.

Hail, B. A., and Duncan, K. C.: *Out of the North: The Subarctic Collection of the Haffenreffer Museum of Anthropology,* Brown University, 1989.

Harrison, J. D.: *Métis: People Between Two Worlds,* The Glentsaw-Alberta Institute in association with Douglas and McIntyre, 1985.

Hodge, F. (Ed.): *Handbook of American Indians North of Mexico,* two vols., BAEB 30; Smithsonian Institution, 1907–10.

Howard, J. H.: *Reprints in Anthropology Vol. 20:The Dakota or Sioux Indians,* J and L Reprint Co., 1980.

———: *Shawnee: The Ceremonialism of a Native American Tribe and its Cultural Background,* Ohio University Press, 1981.

Huck, B.: *Explaining the Fur Trade Routes of North America,* Heartland Press, 2000.

Johnson, M. J.: *Tribes of the Iroquois Confederacy,* "Men at Arms" series No. 395; Osprey Publishing, Ltd, 2003.

King, J. C. H.: *Thunderbird and Lightning: Indian Life in Northeastern North America 1600–1900,* British Museum Publications Ltd., 1982.

Lake-Thom, Bobby: *Spirits of the Earth: A Guide to Native American Symbols, Stories and Ceremonies,* Plume, 1997.

Lyford, C. A.: *The Crafts of the Ojibwa,* "Indian Handicrafts" series, U.S. BIA 1943.

Page, Jack: *In the Hands of the Great Spirit: The 20,000 Year History of American Indians,* The Free Press, 2003.

Paredes, J. A. (Ed.): *Indians of the Southwestern U.S. in the late 20th Century,* Un. Alabama Press, 1992.

Press, Petra, and Sita, Lisa: *Indians of the Northwest: Traditions, History, Legends and Life,* Gareth Stevens, 2000.

Rinaldi, Anne, *My Heart Is on the Ground: The Diary ol Nannie Little Rose, a Sioux Girl, Carlisle Indian School, Pennsylvania, 1880* (Dear American Series), Scholastic Inc., 1999.

Scriver, B.: *The Blackfeet: Artists of the Northern Plains,* The Lowell Press Inc., 1990.

Sita, Lisa: *Indians of the Northeast: Traditions, History, Legends and Life,* Gareth Stevens, 2000.

———: *Indians of the Great Plains: Traditions, History, Legends and Life,* Gareth Stevens, 2000.

———: *Indians of the Southwest: Traditions, History, Legends and Life,* Gareth Stevens, 2000.

Swanton, John R.: *Indian Tribes of the Lower Mississippi Valley and Adjacent Coast of the Gulf of Mexico;* BAEB 43; Smithsonian Institution, 1911.

Early History of the Creek Indians and Their Neighbors; BAEB 73; Smithsonian Institution, 1922.

———: *Indians of the Southeastern United States;* BAEB 137; Smithsonian Institution, 1946.

———: *The Indian Tribes of North America;* BAEB 145; Smithsonian Institution, 1952.

Waldman, Carl: *Atlas of The North American Indian,* Checkmark Books, 2000.

Wright, Muriel H.: *A Guide to the Indian Tribes of Oklahoma,* Un. Oklahoma Press, 1951.

INDEX OF TRIBES

This index cites references to all six volumes of the Native Tribes of North America set, using the following abbreviations for each of the books: GB = Great Basin and Plateau, NE = Northeast, NW = North and Northwest Coast, PP = Plains and Prairie, SE = Southeast, SW = California and the Southwest.

Abenaki: 9, 11, 25, 27, 48, 50, 51, 54, 56 (NE)
Abihka: 34 (SE)
Achomawi (Achumawi): 11, 50, 54 (SW)
Acolapissa: 11, 46, 47, 50 (SE)
Acoma Pueblo: 37, 42, 43, 44 (SW)
Adai: 11, 46, 51 (SE)
Ahtena: 11, 16, (NW)
Aivilingmiut (Aivillirmiut): 30 (NW)
Akokisa: 47 (SE)
Akudnirmiut: 29 (NW)
Alabama and Coushatta: 11, 12–13, 34, 39, 55 (SE)
Alaskan Inuit: 33 (NW)
Aleut: 9, 10, 11, 29, 30, 32, 51 (NW)
Algonkian (Algonquian): 24, 52, 54 (NW); 8, 16, 21, 42, 43, 50 (PP); 6, 8, 9, 10, 12, 13, 15, 25, 26, 27, 28, 29, 30, 32, 40, 41, 42, 47, 48, 50, 51, 52, 53, 54, 55, 56, 57 (NE)
Algonkian–Wakashan: 36 (NW)
Algonkin (Algonquin): 26, 40 (NW); 11, 48 (NE)
Alsea: 21, 53, 57 (NW)
Altamaha: 56–57 (SE)
Anadarko: 49–50 (SE)
Apache: 12, (NW); 42, 45 (GB); 9, 11, 12–21, 30, 44, 47, (SW); 8, 10, 26, 34, 38, 39, 54 (PP)
Apalachee: 11, 36, 39, 42, 46, 48 (SE)
Apalachicola: 48, 50 (SE)
Arapaho: 37, 45 (GB); 7, 8, 9, 10, 11, 12–13, 21, 22, 24, 41, 50 (PP); 48 (NE)
Arikara: 8, 11, 30, 36, 37, 49, 50 (PP)
Arkansea: see Quapaw
Assiniboine: 4, 11, 14,15, 25, 27, 28, 29, 40, 49, (PP)

Atakapa: 11, 26, 46–47, 56 (SE)
Atfalati: 53 (NW)
Athabascan (Athapascan or Athapaskan): 8, 9, 12–20, 25, 28, 31, 33, 41, 48, 53 (NW); 9, 11, 12, 13, 16, 17, 18, 30, 54 (SW); 34 (PP)
Atka: 51 (NW)
Atsina: see Gros Ventre
Atsugewi: see Achomawi
Attikamek: see Tête de Boule

Baffin Island Inuit: 29 (NW)
Bannock: 11, 33, 34, 38, 39, 50 (GB)
Bayogoula: 11, 46, 47 (SE)
Bear Lake: 8, 11 (NW)
Bear River: 13 (NW); 54 (NE)
Beaver: 11, 16, 19, 25 (NW); 38 (NE)
Beaver Hills People: 29 (PP)
Bella Coola: see Nuxalk
Beothuk: 8, 11, 51, 52 (NW)
Biloxi: 11, 47, 53, 54, 55, 56, (SE)
Blackfeet (Blackfoot): 13, 18, 22, 23, 26, 34, 36, 38, (GB); 7, 8, 9, 11, 14, 16-20, 25, 27, 29, 43, 50, 56 (PP)
Brotherton (Brothertown): 11, 13, 14, 26, 50, 52, 53, 54 (NE)
Bungi: see Plains Ojibwa

Caddo: see Kadohadacho
Caddoan: 16 (SW); 38, 50, 52, 56, 57 (PP); 23 (NE); 7, 39, 46, 49, 50–51, 52 (SE)
Cahto: see Kato
Cahuilla: 11, 50, 51, 53 (SW)
Calapooya: 54 (NW)
Calling River: 28 (PP)
Calusa: 11, 39, 47–48 (SE)
Cape Fear Indians: 11, 48 (SE)
Capinans: 47 (SE)

Caribou Inuit: 29, 34 (NW)
Carrier: 11, 16 (NW)
Cascade: see Watlala
Catawba: 11, 14–15, 32, 49 (SE)
Cathlamet: 11, 22 (NW)
Cathlapotle: 11, 23 (NW)
Cayuga: 11, 19, 22, 23, 24, 25, 38 (NE); 56 (SE)
Cayuse: 11, 26, 48, 50, 51, 53, 54, 57 (GB)
Chakchiuma: 11, 48, 50 (SE)
Chastacosta: 11, 12 (NW)
Chatot: 11, 48 (SE)
Chawanoke (Chowanoc): 54 (NE)
Chawasha: 26 (SE)
Chehalis: 11, 21, 22, 42, 43 (NW)
Chelamela: 53 (NW)
Chelan: 11, 51 (GB)
Chemakuan: see Chimakum
Chemehuevi: 31, 32, 33,34 (GB)
Chepenafa: 54 (NW)
Cheraw: 48–49 (SE)
Cherokee: 30 (SW); 8, 11, 14, 23, 49 (NE); 2, 8, 10, 11, 15, 16-23, 31, 32, 33, 36, 39, 41, 49, 51, 57 (SE)
Chetco: 11, 12, 14 (NW); 42 (PP)
Cheyenne: 42, 45 (GB); 7, 8, 10, 11, 12, 13, 21–24, 25, 41, 42, 51 (PP); 14, 48 (NE)
Chickamauga-Cherokee: 19 (SE)
Chickasaw: 8, 10, 11, 17, 24–25, 28, 29, 39, 41, 48, 51, 53 (SE)
Chilcotin: 11, 16–17, 18 (NW)
Chilluckittequaw: 11, 52 (NW)
Chilula and Whilkut: 11, 12 (NW)
Chimakum: 11, 52, 53, 55 (NW)
Chimariko: 11, 50 (SW)

Chinook: 7, 11, 21–23, 42, 43, 47, 52, 56, 57 (NW)
Chinookan: 23 (NW); 49, 57 (GB)
Chipewyan: 11, 25 (NW)
Chippewa: see Ojibwa
Chiricahua Apache: 11, 12–13 (SW)
Chitimacha: 11, 26–27, 32, 47, 54, 55 (SE)
Choctaw: 8, 10, 11, 24, 28–32, 36, 39, 41, 47, 48, 49, 52, 53, 54, 55 (SE)
Chugach (Chugachigniut): 10, 29, 51 (NW)
Chumash: 8, 11, 50–51 (SW)
Clackamas: 11, 23 (NW)
Clallam: 11, 42, 52 (NW)
Clatsop: 11, 22 (NW)
Clowwewalla: 11, 23 (NW)
Coast Rogue groups: 11, 12, 14–15 (NW)
Coast Salish: 7, 22, 23, 42–47 (NW); 12 (GB); 8 (PP)
Cochiti Pueblo: 37–38 (SW)
Cocopa (Cocopah): 11, 46, 47 (SW)
Coeur d'Alene: 11, 12, 26, 49, 50, 51 (GB)
Columbia: see Sinkiuse
Colville: 11, 29, 50, 51, 53, 54, 55, 57 (GB)
Comanche: 36, 39 (GB); 12, 14, 15, 16, 41 (SW); 7, 9, 10, 11, 12, 25–26, 34, 35, 53, 54 (PP)
Comox: 11, 37, 42, 43, 44 (NW)
Conoy: 11, 15, 50, 53 (NE)
Coos: 11, 13, 15, 52, 53 (NW)
Copper Inuit: 30, 34 (NW)
Coquille: 11, 13, 52, 53 (NW)
Costanoan: 7, 11 (SW)
Coushatta: see Alabama
Coweta: 34 (SE)
Cowichan: 42, 43 (NW)

ABOUT THE CONTRIBUTORS

Richard Hook (Illustrator and Contributing Author
An internationally respected professional illustrator specializing in historical and anthropological subjects for more than thirty years, Hook has had a lifelong interest in Native American culture that has inspired his remarkable artwork. He has been widely published in the United States, Europe, and Japan. A lifelong interest in Native American culture led to his selection as illustrator for the Denali Press Award-winning *The Encyclopedia of Native American Tribes*.

Michael G. Johnson (Author)
Johnson has researched the material culture, demography, and linguistic relationships of Native American peoples for more than thirty years, through academic institutions in North America and Europe and during numerous field studies conducted with the cooperation and hospitality of many Native American communities. He has published a number of books, in particular the Denali Press Award-winning *Encyclopedia of Native American Tribes*.